DEDICATION

To all who come to this happy place:

welcome.

Disneyland is your land.

Here, age relives fond memories

of the past,

and here youth may savor

the challenge and promise

of the future.

Disneyland is dedicated

to the ideals, the dreams,

and the hard facts that

have created America . . .

with the hope that it will be a source of joy

and inspiration to all the world.

July 17, 1955

For Disney Editions
Editorial Director: Wendy Lefkon
Associate Editor: Rich Thomas

For Roundtable Press, Inc.
Directors: Susan E. Meyer, Marsha Melnick, Julie Merberg
Editor: John Glenn
Computer Production, Photo Editor, Designer: Steven Rosen

Text: Tim O'Day

This book is dedicated to the Disneyland cast members, Imagineers, Disney Legends, and Disneyland enthusiasts who keep the spirit of Disneyland alive and who, through their passion, dedication, and enthusiasm, ensure that Disneyland will always be the flagship of the Disney theme parks.

A special thanks to Wendy Lefkon of Disney Editions; Steven Rosen, John Glenn, and Susan Meyer of Roundtable Press; Jeff Kurtti, my inspiration; Dave Smith, Robert Tieman, and Rebecca Cline of The Walt Disney Archives; Susie McFarland, Gail Kirkpatrick, Joyce Trent-Morgan, and Glenn Miller of Disneyland; and to my dear Tracy, who will always be the "fairest" to me.

ISBN 0-7868-6604-7

First Edition
2 4 6 8 10 9 7 5 3 1

CONTENTS

INTRODUCTION

There may be newer and larger Disney theme parks throughout the world, but without Walt Disney's personal determination and the initial innovation of Disneyland® Park, these other developments never would have seen reality. Today, Disneyland stands as a living blueprint for all that has come to pass since its opening in 1955. And as the new millennium dawns, the Disneyland Resort will experience its greatest period of growth and excitement, fulfilling Walt Disney's desire that "it will continue to grow as long as there is imagination left in the world."

The story of Disneyland is the story of one man's dream and his journey to see his magic kingdom rise in the orange groves. It is also the story of the over 400 million guests who have visited the park and the dedicated cast members who, through their combined enthusiasm, passion, and loyalty, have made Disneyland a beloved international institution.

It is my hope that this book gives you a greater appreciation for the incredible ongoing story that is Disneyland and that it also rekindles fond memories for you long after you leave the gates of "The Happiest Place on Earth."

Tim O'Day

STROLLING DOWN MEMORY LANE IN "THE HAPPIEST PLACE ON EARTH"

"Disneyland will never be completed as long as there is imagination left in the world"

Walt Disney

1955

▶ After more than 20 years of planning and dreaming, Walt Disney opens the original Disney theme park, Disneyland® Park, to a curious world on Sunday, July 17, 1955.

During its first year of operation, Disneyland presents the following attractions in five themed lands:

Main Street, USA
● Disneyland Railroad
● Horse-drawn Street Cars
● Horse-drawn Fire Wagon
● Main Street Cinema
● Horse-drawn Surreys
● Main Street Penny Arcade
● Main Street Shooting Gallery

Adventureland
● Jungle Cruise

Fantasyland
● King Arthur Carrousel
● Peter Pan Flight
● Mr. Toad's Wild Ride
● Canal Boats of the World
● Snow White's Adventures
● Casey Jr. Circus Train
● Dumbo the Flying Elephant
● Mickey Mouse Club Theater
● Mickey Mouse Club Circus
● Mad Tea Party

Frontierland
● Stage Coach
● Mule Pack
● Mark Twain Riverboat
● Golden Horseshoe Revue
● Davy Crockett Museum
● Conestoga Wagons
● Mike Fink Keel Boats

Tomorrowland
● Tomorrowland Autopia
● Space Station X-1
● Circarama, USA (360-degree film, *A Tour of the West*)
● Monsanto Hall of Chemistry
● Rocket to the Moon
● Phantom Boats
● Color Gallery
● The World Beneath Us
● 20,000 Leagues Under the Sea
● Tomorrowland Flight Circle
● Aluminum Hall of Fame

1956

▶ On September 8, after only seven weeks of operation, Disneyland welcomes Elsa Marquez as its one millionth guest.

▶ The "Fantasy in the Sky" fireworks spectacular is introduced

▶ 15 new attractions are added to Disneyland:

● Astro Jets
● Bathroom of Tomorrow
● Storybook Land Canal Boats
● Tom Sawyer Island Rafts
● Skyway to Tomorrowland and Skyway to Fantasyland
● Horseless Carriages (red and yellow)
● Rainbow Ridge Pack Mules
● Rainbow Mountain
● Stage Coach
● Rainbow Caverns
● Mine Train
● Main Street Omnibus
● Indian Village
● Indian War Canoes
● Junior Autopia

1957

▶ Nine new attractions are added to Disneyland:

● Midget Autopia
● Sleeping Beauty Castle (walk-through attraction)
● Holidayland
● Monsanto House of the Future
● Viewliner
● Motor Boat Cruise
● Indian Village Rafts
● Frontierland Shooting Gallery
● Main Street Omnibus

1958

▶ Four new attractions are added to Disneyland:

● Grand Canyon Diorama
● Alice in Wonderland
● Columbia Sailing Ship
● Motorized Main Street Fire Truck

1959

▶ Four new attractions are added to Disneyland:

● Fantasyland Autopia
● Submarine Voyage
● Disneyland-Alweg Monorail System
● Matterhorn Bobsleds

▶ Disneyland greets its 15 millionth guest in April.

1960

▶ Six new attractions are added to Disneyland:

● Main Street Electric Cars
● Art of Animation Exhibit
● Mine Train Through Nature's Wonderland
● Skull Rock
● Pirate's Cove
● New Circarama film *America the Beautiful*

▶ "Dixieland at Disneyland" debuts on the Rivers of America in Frontierland.

1961

▶ Four new attractions are added to Disneyland:

● Snow White Grotto & Wishing Well
● Monorail to Disneyland Hotel
● Flying Saucers
● Babes in Toyland Exhibit

▶ First all-night Grad Nite Party for highschool graduates is held at Disneyland in June.

1962

▶ Four new attractions are added to Disneyland:

● Safari Shooting Gallery
● Indian Village (expansion)
● Jungle Cruise (new scenes added)
● Swiss Family Treehouse

1963

▶ The debut of Walt Disney's Enchanted Tiki Room in Adventureland marks a new era in Disneyland attractions by introducing a new form of three-dimensional animation called Audio-Animatronics®.

▶ The "Parade of Toys" becomes a daily feature during the Christmas holiday.

▶ "Salute to Mexico," a cultural exhibit, is presented by People-to-People and the Mexican Tourist Association.

▶ Disneyland showcases its first "Cavalcade of Big Bands," a series of concerts by some of the biggest names in swing music

1966

► Three major new attractions are added to Disneyland:

- "it's a small world"
- Primeval World Diorama
- New Orleans Square

► In July, Walt Disney dedicates the first new land since the opening of Disneyland—New Orleans Square. This three-acre, $18 million dollar expansion captures the charm of the "Paris of the American Frontier" as it was during the early part of the 18th century.

1965

► The first Disneyland Ambassador to the World, Julie Reihm (chosen in 1964), represents Disneyland® Park on goodwill tours to Europe, Canada, Australia, New Zealand, Japan, and throughout the United States.

► Great Moments with Mr. Lincoln becomes the first Disney show from the 1964-65 New York World's Fair to be transplanted to Disneyland. The show finds a new home in the Main Street Opera House.

1964

► On May 17, "Disneyland Goes to the World's Fair" airs for the first time on Disney's Sunday night TV series *The Wonderful World of Color*. Hosted by Walt Disney, the episode highlights the four Disney shows in the 1964-65 New York World's Fair.

► Two new additions are made to Disneyland:

- Columbia Sailing Ship (below decks museum)
- Jungle Cruise (new scenes added)

1967

► Seven major new attractions are added to Disneyland:

- Pirates of the Caribbean
- Circle-Vision featuring *America the Beautiful*
- Carousel of Progress
- PeopleMover
- Rocket Jets
- Flight to the Moon
- Adventure Thru Inner Space

► In July, 1,500 celebrities and invited guests attend the dedication of an all-new Tomorrowland, revamped at a cost of $23 million. "A World on the Move," Tomorrowland adds six new attractions to the Disneyland landscape.

1968

► Special events for the year include the park's first St. Patrick's Day Parade, first Cinco de Mayo Fiesta, plus a Valentine's Day Party, Spring Fling, Easter Parade, and Angels-Disneyland Fun Day Double-header.

1971

► On October 1, the Walt Disney World® Resort in Florida is officially dedicated and opened by Roy Disney (Walt Disney's brother and lifelong business partner). This new venture in Disney outdoor entertainment is built upon the successful blueprint of Disneyland. Numerous Disneyland cast members in California contribute to the creation and opening of the Walt Disney World Resort.

► Miss Valerie Suldo, a 22-year-old New Brunswick, New Jersey payroll clerk, becomes Disneyland Guest Number 100 million at 11:13 A.M. on Thursday, June 17, 1971, launching a summer-long celebration.

1970

► On July 17, 130 of the original Disneyland staff, known as Club 55, gather for a special celebration. Combined, the total service to Disneyland guests of these very special cast members is more than 1,950 years!

1969

► On August 9, Disneyland officially opens the doors to The Haunted Mansion, one of the park's most beloved attractions.

► "Love Bug Day" is celebrated at Disneyland with the convergence of hundreds of Volkswagens.

► The landing of Apollo 11, on August 12, on the surface of the moon is televised from the Tomorrowland Stage to a throng of fascinated Disneyland guests. This is a historic milestone for Disneyland as well as the world.

► One new attraction is added to Disneyland:

- Davy Crockett's Explorer Canoes (redesigned)

1972

► Disneyland debuts its seventh themed land with the opening of Bear Country and the addition of the following attractions:

- Country Bear Jamboree
- Teddi Bara's Swingin' Arcade

► The beloved "Disneyland Main Street Electrical Parade" premiers at Disneyland and quickly becomes the most popular parade ever staged at a Disney theme park.

1974

► America Sings debuts on June 28 in Tomorrowland's Carousel Theater. This comical, lively, and tune-filled musical showcases nearly 200 years of our nation's musical heritage.

► On July 11, 1974, Disneyland is the star of the nationally televised TV special *Herbie Day at Disneyland*.

1973

► Two new attractions are added to Disneyland:

- The Walt Disney Story
- Disneyland Showcase

► In April, Mrs. Lillian Bounds Disney (Mrs. Walt Disney) officiates at the grand opening of The Walt Disney Story at the Main Street Opera House on Main Street, USA. This impressive and emotional salute to Walt Disney and his creative legacy features exacting recreations of his studio offices, displays of his many awards, and demonstrations of Audio-Animatronics®.

1975

▶ Two new additions are made to Disneyland® Park:

● Mission to Mars
● The Walt Disney Story Featuring Great Moments with Mr. Lincoln (expansion)

▶ Conceived as a salute and celebration in honor of the American Bicentennial, "America on Parade" begins its daily performances in July, 1975, at both Disneyland and at the Walt Disney World Resort, and continues until September, 1976. In all, the red, white, and blue procession completes more than 1,200 performances before a total audience of 25 million guests, the largest audience ever to view a live performance.

1976

▶ On June 22, Elsie Mae Houck of Tulare, California, becomes Disneyland's 150 millionth guest.

▶ Disneyland is the star of two nationally televised TV specials: *Monsanto presents Walt Disney's America on Parade*, starring comedian Red Skelton and airing on April 3, 1976; and *Christmas in Disneyland*, starring actor-comedian Art Carney and airing on December 6, 1976 (this special is famous for its spectacular ice-skating sequence on Main Street, USA).

1978

▶ Disneyland's mighty Matterhorn Bobsleds receives a major renovation which results in the addition of ice caverns, glowing ice crystals, and the ever-threatening Abominable Snowman.

▶ On November 18–19, Mickey's Official 50th Birthday Party is attended by more than 91,762 guests! On hand for the festivities are the original members of *The Mickey Mouse Club*, including Annette Funicello.

1977

▶ At the opening ceremonies of Space Mountain on May 27, Disneyland is honored to have as special guests America's first men in space—the U.S. Mercury Astronauts:

● Scott Carpenter
● Wally Schirra
● U.S. Senator John Glenn
● Betty Grissom, widow of Virgil I. "Gus" Grissom

● Gordon Cooper
● Alan Shepard
● Donald "Deke" Slayton

1982

▶ Beginning in June, the Disneyland Passport, good for admission and unlimited use of park attractions, becomes the exclusive ticket media for the park. With the introduction of the Passport, the venerable Disneyland Ticket Book and its famous A, B, C, D, and E ticket coupons is officially retired.

▶ In July, the Disneyland Marching Band celebrates its 50,000th performance for Disneyland guests.

1985

▶ Two new additions are made to Disneyland:

● Frontierland Shootin' Arcade
● Videopolis

▶ In January, Disneyland kicks off a yearlong celebration of "30 Years of Magic" with daily shows and special parades.
▶ On February 2, the nationally televised TV special *Disneyland's 30th Anniversary Celebration* showcases 30 years of Disneyland.
▶ On February 6, for the first time in its history, Disneyland begins year-round, seven-days-a-week operation.
▶ On August 4, Disneyland welcomes its 250 millionth guest, Brooks Charles Arthur Burr, 3, of Anchorage, Alaska.

1979

▶ On a busy July 4, near Main Street, USA, Teresa Salcedo is born to Rosa and Elias Salcedo of Los Angeles, California. Mickey Mouse later presents little Teresa with Disneyland Birth Certificate No. 1, recognizing the unprecedented event.
▶ In September, Big Thunder Mountain Railroad opens in Frontierland. Replacing the Mine Train Through Nature's Wonderland, the new attraction covers two acres. Huge cranes were used to hoist the complete upper buttes (weighing up to 28 tons) into position atop the massive steel framework.

1981

▶ On January 8, at 11:00 A.M., Gert Schelvis, 26, of Santa Barbara, California, becomes the 200 millionth guest to visit Disneyland.

1980

▶ In January, Disneyland begins its yearlong silver anniversary celebration in grand style with a daily parade, "Disneyland's 25th Anniversary Parade," and the popular stage show "Disneyland is Your Land."

1983

▶ On May 25, an all-new redesigned Fantasyland is unveiled in a spectacular grand opening, including a ceremonial lowering of the Sleeping Beauty Castle drawbridge (an event not seen since the opening day of Disneyland 28 years earlier). The new Fantasyland features new versions of favorite attractions and new landmarks such as:

● Pinocchio's Daring Journey
● Snow White's Scary Adventures
● Peter Pan's Flight
● Mr. Toad's Wild Ride
● Dumbo the Flying Elephant
● The Sword in the Stone
● Mad Tea Party
● King Arthur Carrousel

1984

▶ Three major new attractions are added to Disneyland:

● Alice In Wonderland
● Magic Journeys
● Country Bear Christmas Show

1986

▶ Three major new attractions are added to Disneyland:

● Country Bear Vacation Hoedown
● Big Thunder Ranch
● Magic Eye Theater (featuring *Captain EO*)

▶ Summer sees a total of 1,320 Disneyland cast members and Disney characters join hands in the coast-to-coast charity fundraising effort "Hands Across America."

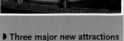

1992

▶ On May 13, Fantasmic!, a new tradition in Disneyland nighttime entertainment, premiers on the Rivers of America in Frontierland. This hugely popular evening extravaganza features a battle of good and evil inside Mickey Mouse's fanciful imagination.

1993

▶ On January 26, Disneyland celebrates the grand opening of Mickey's Toontown, a new addition to Fantasyland. This new area features the following attractions:

● Mickey's House and Movie Barn
● Minnie's House and Garden
● Donald's Boat—The *Miss Daisy*
● Goofy's Bounce House
● Gadget's Go-Coaster
● Jolly Trolley
● Chip 'n Dale's Treehouse

1994

▶ The fun-filled attraction Roger Rabbit's Car Toon Spin officially opens in Mickey's Toontown on January 26.

1987

▶ Two major new attractions are added to Disneyland® Park:

● Star Tours
● The Disney Gallery

▶ On January 12, Star Tours, the first attraction collaboration between Disney and Lucasfilm, Ltd., premieres in Tomorrowland.

1991

▶ In March, Small World Mall is magically transformed into "Disney Afternoon Avenue." Teeming with new sights and sounds, "Disney Afternoon Avenue" gives children a colorful play area in which they can interact with their favorite stars from *The Disney Afternoon* TV series. Highlights include the "Plane Crazy" stage show at Videopolis, and a chance to meet its star, Baloo, in his dressing room.

1998

▶ Michael Eisner, chairman of the board and chief executive officer of The Walt Disney Company, officially dedicates the new Tomorrowland, along with 40 past and present U.S. Astronauts, on Thursday, May 21.

1999

▶ On May 20, Disneyland hosts the official homecoming of Army Staff Sergeant Andrew Ramirez, Staff Sergeant Christopher Stone, and Specialist Steven Gozales. It is the first time the three U.S. soldiers, who had been captured by Serbian forces on March 31, stand on American soil since their release from captivity.

2000

▶ In January, Disneyland kicks off a yearlong celebration of its 45th birthday.

● Tarzan's Treehouse™ opens in Adventureland on June 23 (replacing the Swiss Family Treehouse).

1995

▶ In February, the biggest attraction ever created for a Disney theme park—The Indiana Jones™ Adventure—is unveiled during a star-studded opening gala.

1990

▶ The 35th anniversary of Disneyland is marked by the premiere of the "Party Gras Parade," featuring wild and fun Latin beats and six 37-foot-tall Disney character inflatable balloon floats.

1997

▶ On August 1, Bob Penfield, the last of the original Disneyland opening day cast members, retires after more than 42 years of service. To commemorate this special occasion, Bob is honored with a window on Main Street displaying the legend "Club 55 School of Golf, Bob Penfield, Instructor."

▶ "it's a small world" Holiday premiers on November 27. This all-new winter holiday-theme overlay to the classic Disneyland attraction "it's a small world" highlights winter holiday festivities around the world and intertwines "Deck the Halls" and "Jingle Bells" with the attraction's famous theme song.

1996

▶ Springtime sees the transformation of Big Thunder Ranch into the medieval setting of "The Hunchback of Notre Dame Festival of Fools." This popular stage show, presented in the round, is derived from the Disney animated film *The Hunchback of Notre Dame*.

1989

▶ On July 17, Splash Mountain, the most elaborate flume attraction in the world, opens to Disneyland guests. Located in Critter Country (formerly Bear Country), the towering 87-foot-tall Splash Mountain adventure culminates in a breathtaking five-story drop at a 45-degree angle. Splash Mountain is based upon the animated sequences of Walt Disney's classic 1946 film *Song of the South*.

1988

▶ Mickey's 60th birthday is celebrated daily during the summer with "Mickey's 60th Birthday Parade" and "Mickey's Birthday Bash" in the Plaza Hub.

▶ On May 5, Disney Dollars are unveiled at Disneyland. This unique currency, with equivalent value to U.S. currency, is introduced for use at the Disney theme parks and resorts. Mickey Mouse appears on the $1 bill and Goofy on the $5 bill. A $10 bill featuring Minnie Mouse is added on November 20, 1989.

▶ In the spring, "Blast to the Past" premieres, a whimsical look at the fads and fancies of the 1950s.
▶ As part of "Blast to the Past," Disneyland stages the Super Hooper Duper on March 25. This gathering of 1,527 energetic hula-hoopers in front of Sleeping Beauty Castle smashes the world's record for the most persons hula-hooping at one time in one location.

THE JOURNEY BEGINS

The creation of Disneyland® Park is perhaps the single greatest example of Walt Disney's genius.  Building on his personal and professional experiences, Walt Disney conceived one of the most important entertainment landmarks of the 20th century—a place that transcends age, language, and politics. Disneyland has become a living blueprint for all the Disney theme parks and resorts that have followed its successful example. The story of Disneyland is very much a journey, so rewind your Mickey Mouse watch back about 45 years and let the journey begin . . .

A Magical Little Park

In the late 1940s tourism was fast becoming an important industry in California. Studies showed that visitors to Southern California simply wanted to see the Pacific Ocean, pick an orange from the then-abundant orange farms, and visit a real Hollywood movie studio.

"You know, it's a shame people come to Hollywood and find there's nothing to see," Walt Disney commented at the time. "Even the people who come to the [Disney] studio. What do they see? A bunch of guys bending over drawings. Wouldn't it be nice if people could come to Hollywood and see something?"

Walt Disney had been thinking about giving the curious public something to see since the mid-1930s. Inspired both by the general public's interest in the movies and the "kiddie parks" to which he often took his children, Walt wondered if his studio could construct a park that would combine the two. "When I built the studio," he recalled, "I thought we ought to have a three-dimensional thing that people could actually come and visit—they can't visit our studio because the rooms are small."

But Depression-era investors were shy of the risks involved in what Walt called his "little dream," and he couldn't get anybody to go in with him. Even his brother and partner, Roy O. Disney, co-founder of The Walt Disney Company, was resistant. "Whenever I'd go down and talk to my brother about it, why he'd always suddenly get busy with some figures so, I mean, I didn't dare bring it up," Walt would recall in later years.

Walt's idea for "a magical little park" went through many modifications over the years. In the beginning, he imagined a modest little playground—"Mickey Mouse Park"—built on the studio lot in Burbank, California, that would feature rides and amusements themed around popular Disney characters. The idea, though, never really got beyond the talking stages and the little park continued to evolve in his imagination. By the end of World War II, Walt's vision had grown in both size and substance, influenced by a reawakened interest in a childhood hobby—trains.

As a little boy growing up in the Midwest, Walt had been fascinated by trains. So when his doctor suggested that he pursue a hobby to relieve the stress of running his studio, Walt returned to his boyhood passion for railroading.

Coincidentally, two of Disney's top animators, Ward Kimball and Ollie Johnston, were also serious train hobbyists. Walt consulted both of them as he constructed his own train engine—a one-eighth scale model of a 19th-century Southern Pacific Railroad locomotive. Walt built many of the engine's components with his own hands and dubbed the engine the *Lilly Belle,* after his wife Lillian.

From one engine the hobby soon grew to consume the backyard of Walt's new home, then under construction. With layouts in hand, Walt set out to construct an entire miniature railroad, his beloved Carolwood Pacific Railroad (named for his new home address in Holmby Hills, California). The only obstacle was Lillian and her own plans for their backyard. Unfortunately, a section of the track was slated to run right through her proposed flower garden. After promising to build a tunnel under her garden, Walt secured approval from his wife in the form of a humorous mock contract.

Walt Disney fires up the *Lilly Belle* to full steam, much to the delight of his young passengers (above).

Guests to the Main Street Station at Disneyland® Park can see the original *Lilly Belle* on display (opposite page), along with vintage photographs of Walt and his fellow railroading enthusiasts enjoying their hobby.

On May 15, 1950, the *Lilly Belle* made its debut as part of the Carolwood Pacific Railroad, huffing and puffing its way over trestles and through tunnels in Walt and Lillian's backyard. The personal satisfaction and joy Walt derived from his railroading hobby influenced his "magical little park" concept. The idea of a playground in a corner of the studio property, which would naturally incorporate a train, kept rolling around in his mind.

Meanwhile, Walt's interests expanded to include a fascination with mechanical miniatures. He made plans for a traveling exhibit called "Disneylandia," which would consist of custom-crafted, mechanically activated miniatures similar to the automatons of centuries past. They would bring to life American history and folklore through the use of elaborate stage sets. However, a revenue analysis proved that such an exhibit would not be cost-effective and the idea was shelved.

Undeterred, Walt incorporated the Disneylandia concept in his evolving notion of a kiddie park with a train. In addition to a possible display of Walt's mechanized miniatures, the new park would feature a carousel, a large lake, a bird island, a Mississippi steamboat, a fairground, picnic areas, statues of the Disney characters, and, of course, a steam train. The park would be rooted in Walt's philosophy of building a place where "parents and children could have fun together." A 16-acre parcel of land across the street from the Walt Disney Studios (and bordering the Los Angeles River) seemed the ideal location for Walt's long-sought dream.

Roy Disney, however, was not initially enthusiastic about Walt's plans. As the chief financial officer for the company, Roy had the responsibility of managing the funds supporting Walt's creative endeavors. Roy approached this new idea with his usual caution. He reminded Walt that they were still in the movie business and that their fortunes rode on the success of their films.

Walt prevailed: in 1952 Roy put together a budget allocation of $10,000 for the development of the park idea. The budget estimate, however, was quickly made obsolete by the ever-increasing scope of Walt's plans, which outgrew the proposed location (now part of the Ventura Freeway and Walt Disney Feature Animation headquarters). The more Walt thought about the park, the grander and more elaborate his plans became.

Support for Walt's vision was tepid outside the Walt Disney Studios. The expected cooperation from the Burbank City Council did not materialize, and many people wondered why Disney would want to get involved in the amusement park business anyway—with its unsavory reputation and lack of sophistication.

Walt even fielded the same query from his wife Lillian. "Why would you want to get involved with an amusement park?" she asked. "They're so dirty and not fun at all for grown-ups. Why would you want to get involved in a business like that?" Walt responded with his usual enthusiasm: "That's exactly my point," he exclaimed. "Mine isn't going to be that way. Mine's going to be a place that's clean, where the whole family can do things together."

DISNEYLAND

Imagineering a Masterpiece

Walt Disney's failure to secure support for his idea for a park across the street from the Disney studio on Riverside Drive, and the inadequacy of the $10,000 that his brother Roy had allocated for research and development of the concept, left him more determined than ever to see his park built.

Walt knew that he would require a lot more money to make his dream a reality. So he sold his family vacation home in Palm Springs and borrowed against his life insurance policy to raise the funds necessary to keep progress on the park moving swiftly forward.

With seed money in hand, Walt considered hiring an outside architectural firm to create Disneyland® Park. He decided, though, that outside architects would not have the show-business orientation or entertainment experience his project would require. At the suggestion of a friend, Walt realized that he already possessed a creative team at the studio whose talents he could call upon—a team steeped in the Disney way of creating entertainment.

In December 1952, Walt gathered together a stellar group of designers, architects, writers, sculptors, engineers, craftsmen, and special-effects experts from both inside his studio and from outside firms. This group formed the original staff of WED Enterprises (WED is an acronym for Walter Elias Disney), Walt's privately owned design and engineering firm. Their first assignment was to create Disneyland from scratch. (WED became Walt Disney Imagineering, or WDI, in 1986 and has designed and built every Disney theme park and resort around the world).

"All I want you to think about is that when people walk through or ride through or have access to anything that you design, I want them, when they leave, to have a smile on their face," Walt instructed his Imagineers. "Just remember that. That's all I ask of you as a designer."

Now the daunting process of generating ideas for Disneyland® Park and then developing the means to realize them could begin in earnest. Walt's creative team was in essence a team of dreamers and doers, with Walt acting as head contributor, coach, and booster. The atmosphere at WED was filled with the spirit of innovation, collaboration, and enthusiasm.

The first solid, comprehensive view of the Disneyland concept was swept into being one Saturday in September 1953. Roy Disney, scheduled to travel to New York City to secure funding for the project, needed an impressive visualization of the park to show prospective investors. Working over the weekend at his studio with Herb Ryman, a noted artist and former Disney art director, Walt conjured up the first coherent view of Disneyland as we know it today.

Walt's team of Imagineers then used Ryman's large pencil aerial schematic to forge a cohesive vision out of their disparate ideas and concepts. From a mountain of drawings, renderings, and blueprints emerged the original layout of Disneyland.

The first written concept for the park states that "Disneyland will be something of a fair, an exhibition, a playground, a community center, a museum of living facts, and a showplace of beauty and magic. It will be filled with the accomplishments, the joys and hopes of the world we live in. And it will remind us and show us how to make these wonders part of our own lives."

The design and layout of Disneyland reflected Walt's personal interests and, in turn, his instinct for what he thought his guests would enjoy experiencing firsthand. Main Street, the main entrance corridor of the park, was inspired by Walt's memories of Marceline, Missouri, where he lived from 1906 to 1911 between the ages of 4 and 9, and which he considered his hometown. Everyone has a place they like to think of as their hometown and Main Street, reminiscent of a typical midwestern small town circa 1910, is a nostalgic hometown for everyone.

This aerial schematic of Disneyland, as rendered by legendary Disney Imagineer Herb Ryman, was the very first visualization of the Disneyland concept (opposite page).

Walt Disney points out features of his Magic Kingdom on a rendering created by famed Disney artist Peter Ellenshaw (right). The artwork was highlighted in the very first episode of the *Disneyland* TV show.

At the end of Main Street guests would find themselves in the Plaza Hub. From this central location they could enter any one of the main "themed" lands, each of which reflected Walt's personal enthusiasms. His pride in U.S. history and the legends of the American frontier could be found in Frontierland. His life-long fascination with nature would help bring his popular "True-Life Adventures" film series to life in Adventureland. The fanciful characters and locales of his beloved animated films would be realized in Fantasyland, and his dreams for a better future through emerging technologies could be found in Tomorrowland.

Walt and his Imagineers were literally creating an entirely new concept in outdoor entertainment—the very first theme park. Their concepts, designs, and plans forever changed the face of outdoor recreation and created the blueprint for today's modern shopping malls and themed restaurants.

As innovative and groundbreaking as Disneyland® Park may have been, it was soon derided by naysayers who forecasted disaster for Walt's new venture. Skepticism about Disneyland ran high throughout Hollywood—Disney business associates could not understand Walt's desire for an amusement park.

"Almost everyone warned us that Disneyland would be a Hollywood spectacular— a spectacular failure," Walt once recalled. "But they were thinking about an amusement park, and we believed in our idea—a family park where parents and children could have fun together."

Whether or not failure was to result, the planning for Disneyland proceeded and Walt's vision came closer to concrete reality with each passing day. Soon the search was on to quickly identify the ideal location for the project. As early as 1952 Disney staff members began secretly scouting possible areas throughout Southern California.

One of the first sites considered was the Los Angeles Police pistol range in the city of Chatsworth. Its appeal lay in its rural setting and easy access to the surrounding developing suburbs of Los Angeles. Eventually this site became a decoy to throw off land speculators. Other locations were researched and discarded.

Walt grew frustrated with his haphazard search. In 1953 he retained the services of Stanford Research Institute to conduct feasibility studies. Their initial findings concluded that the concept for the park was a good idea, considering the fact that tourism was California's third largest industry. The studies also provided critical information concerning population trends, topography, roadway and freeway access, utilities, taxes, local government support, and building code requirements. More than 40 different potential sites were earmarked for research.

As the search gathered momentum, more and more people became aware of what was happening and Walt's project was becoming less of a secret. Pressure to maintain the secrecy of the project mounted when Disney entered negotiations with 17 families who owned a series of orange groves in a quiet rural community called Anaheim.

Located 40 miles south of downtown Los Angeles in Orange County, Anaheim was predicted to become the population center for Southern California's eight growing counties (the actual geo-population center of Southern California is today only four miles from the actual site of the Disneyland® Resort—a very accurate prediction).

The site in Anaheim was attractive for its proximity to the major metropolitan areas of Los Angeles, which would be made even more accessible by the soon-to-be-completed Santa Ana Freeway. Orange County's temperate climate and reasonable land values were also ideal.

In August 1953, 160 acres of orange groves in Anaheim were selected as the home for Disneyland® Park. The news was kept quiet until the *Anaheim Bulletin* newspaper broke the story on May 1, 1954. The site was perfect—160 acres of flat land from which Walt Disney and his staff could excavate rivers, mold mountains, plant forests and jungles, and erect small towns, rockets, and castles. There was enough land to greatly expand upon the initial concepts originally envisioned a few years earlier for the magical little park in Burbank.

On July 21, 1954, Walt Disney broke ground for Disneyland. Only 257 working days remained until the scheduled opening of the park on July 17, 1955. The final countdown to the reality of his long-sought dream had begun.

Herb Ryman's early rendering of Sleeping Beauty Castle at the entrance to Fantasyland (opposite page).

Walt Disney poses with the original model of Sleeping Beauty Castle (left).

Building a Dream On Air

While Walt and his Imagineers grappled with the creative aspects of Disneyland® Park, Roy Disney had the difficult task of finding the money to fund his younger brother's big dream. It's indicative of the resourcefulness and trend-bucking nature of the Disney brothers that they would consider a source of financing many of their Hollywood colleagues viewed as the enemy: television.

In the early 1950s the medium of television was in its infancy and the three major networks were eager to add big-name talent to their roster of shows. Most of Hollywood resented television, but not Walt. After the success of his first TV special, *One Hour in Wonderland* in 1950, Walt regarded TV as an ally in promoting his films and characters. Soon the networks were courting him for a weekly television series.

"Every time I'd get to thinking of television I would think of this park," Walt once explained. "And I knew that if I did anything like the park that I would have to have some kind of a medium like television to let the people know about it."

With Herb Ryman's sketch of the park in hand, along with Walt's original concept treatment, Roy Disney flew to New York City in September 1953 to visit the major TV networks and gauge their interest in a weekly Disney TV show—and Disneyland. The networks couldn't understand Walt's insistence on their funding Disneyland as part of any agreement involving Disney's commitment to a weekly TV show. After one particularly impressive presentation, though, Roy secured a seven-year contract with ABC for a weekly TV show in exchange for initial financial backing of Disneyland.

The television show, hosted by Walt Disney himself, was to be called *Disneyland* and the subject matter of each show would be derived from one of the four main

realms of the park. There would be the true stories and legends of pioneer America from Frontierland, stories set in exotic locales and True-Life Adventure films from Adventureland, tales of fantasy and whimsy from Fantasyland, and visions of things to come from Tomorrowland.

The *Disneyland* show was the perfect forum for Walt to explain his new venture to a curious public, while providing entertaining programming as well. Beginning with the first episode, aired on October 27, 1954, Walt took his viewers on a behind-the-scenes tour of his dream-in-progress. Subsequent episodes would continue to provide updates of the construction at the park.

It was a success from the beginning. In December 1954, the *Disneyland* TV series created a sensation with the premiere of the first of three episodes highlighting the tales of legendary frontiersman Davy Crockett. The shows, which consisted of "Davy Crockett: Indian Fighter," "Davy Crockett Goes to Congress," and "Davy Crockett at the Alamo," caused a national craze among youngsters across America. Coonskin caps became all the fashion and "The Ballad of Davy Crockett" climbed to the top of the "Hit Parade" charts. At the end of its first season, the *Disneyland* show won an Emmy Award as Best Variety Series, followed the next year by another award for Walt Disney as Best Producer of a Filmed Series.

The tremendous popular acclaim for the *Disneyland* series, and the Davy Crockett episodes in particular, led Walt to produce another show for ABC—*The Mickey Mouse Club*. This new series debuted on October 3, 1955, and quickly became one of the most beloved children's TV series of all time.

Due to their immense popularity, elements from both the Davy Crockett shows and *The Mickey Mouse Club* would eventually be integrated into Disneyland® Park, with performers from each show participating in the grand opening festivities in 1955.

Now that financial backing for his park seemed secure, thanks to ABC and the success of his weekly show, Walt was busier than he had ever been in his entire career. While venturing into television (and becoming a household name and instant celebrity), he continued to oversee all film production at the studio in addition to the creation of Disneyland. It was truly an exciting era for Walt as he drew closer to raising the curtain on something completely new and unique—the very first Disney theme park.

A Magic Kingdom Rises
in the Orange Groves

Funding secured and plans in hand, Walt was now in an enviable but anxious position: he must make good on all the creative and financial commitments he had entered into in order to transform his dream of Disneyland® Park into three-dimensional reality. With TV shows to produce in addition to traditional movie offerings—and with virtually every department also participating in some way in the creation of the park—activity at Walt Disney Studio exploded.

Every available office and meeting space was devoted to either the creation of Disney's next two animated features (*Lady and the Tramp* and *Sleeping Beauty*), the *Disneyland* TV series, or Disneyland itself. Soundstages on the studio lot were converted from movie-making venues to Imagineering departments.

One of the larger soundstages was host to a remarkable sight—the construction of the superstructure of the first stern-wheel steamboat to be built in the United States in over half a

Curious guests to the Disneyland construction site check progress on the Main Street Train Station and the soon-to-be planted floral Mickey (opposite page).

Famed Sleeping Beauty Castle takes shape beneath the construction catwalks and scaffolding (above).

Main Street begins to take shape with the construction of the Market House and Greeting Card Shop (top).

The original Moonliner Rocket is readied for its permanent "launch" site in Tomorrowland (middle).

Victorian Main Street décor contrasts with the jungle themes of Adventureland during construction of buildings facing the Plaza Hub (bottom).

century, the triple-deck paddle wheeler *Mark Twain.* Destined to ply the muddy waters of the Rivers of America in Frontierland, the *Mark Twain* was the first ever prefabricated stern-wheeler—constructed in sections and transported to Disneyland® Park in pieces.

Other studio soundstages and workshops were soon filled with giant teacups, mechanized exotic animals, pieces of a rocket ship, castle turrets, steam train parts, miniature cars, and props, signage, and décor of every kind. A number of the original attractions for Disneyland were constructed at Walt Disney Studio in Burbank and transported to Anaheim.

During these hectic days of preparation for the fast-approaching opening of the park, Walt seemed to thrive on the energy, excitement, and activity. Dividing his time between the construction site in Anaheim and the soundstages of his studio, he seemed to be everywhere, checking up on every little detail.

As construction of the park began, one of the first elements to be created was a 15-foot-high elevated berm surrounding the site. "I don't want the public to see the world they live in while they're in the park," Walt Disney commented. "I want them to feel they're in another world."

Soon the tracks of the Disneyland Railroad were laid around the completed berm, with many of the Main Street buildings going up shortly after. In designing Main Street, the Imagineers added an element of whimsy to the look of the buildings by making all of them slightly smaller than they appear to be, an old trick borrowed from their movie-making roots.

The Main Street Fire Station, located in Town Square, was among the first buildings constructed on the site. The little Fire Station is significant because it houses a small studio apartment upstairs, where Walt occasionally spent the night during construction. It also had a functional fire pole via which Walt and his guests could exit. The apartment is maintained to this day in the Victorian décor he and Lillian used to decorate it. Disneyland old-timers still recall with fondness that it was not unusual to find Walt up early in the morning wandering the park in his bathrobe, inspecting progress on every aspect of the construction.

Despite Walt's constant attention, the building of Disneyland was not without its problems and frustrations. In addition to working with construction crews unaccustomed to creating unique structures such as log stockades, stone castles, and thatched huts, the Imagineers had to deal with a daily dose of the unexpected.

When the time came to first fill the Rivers of America in Frontierland with water, the Imagineers watched in amazement as the water quickly seeped away into the loose soil of

As seen in this aerial photograph, what was once a series of privately-owned orange groves is quickly being transformed into the very first Disney theme park (above).

Many Disney old-timers recall how Walt Disney seemed to be everywhere during construction of the park. Here he inspects one of the engines of the Disneyland Railroad with the help of a familiar little personality (left).

Walt Disney inspects the authentically constructed log stockade at the entrance to Frontierland (right). Even after the park's completion, it was not uncommon to find Walt surveying progress on the park in the early morning hours before it opened to the public. Here he monitors work on the Main Street trolley tracks in the early formative years of the park (opposite page).

28

the former citrus grove. Before they would risk refilling it, the Imagineers had the entire riverbed encased with a local nonporous clay that could hold back the water.

Another concern was landscaping. Due to tight budget constraints, Walt wanted to save as many of the existing trees on the property as was practical. Each tree was tagged with a different colored ribbon to identify its fate—"move," "remove," or "save." Unfortunately, most of the trees were accidentally bulldozed—it was discovered later that the bulldozer operator was color blind.

Nonetheless, the Disney landscape architects nearly depleted nurseries from Santa Barbara to San Diego, searching for just the right types of vegetation to bring the park's different areas to life. Beautiful olive trees and magnolias were found for Main Street; pines, oaks, birches, and maples were located for Frontierland; and a variety of exotic tropical plants were discovered for Adventureland.

Construction on Disneyland® Park continued all the way up to the morning of the grand opening. Last-minute details coupled with increasing costs and dwindling funds fueled rumors that Disneyland would be "Disney's Folly." However, Walt, with his usual confidence and enthusiasm, saw the project differently.

"It's no secret that we were sticking just about every nickel we had on the chance that people would really be interested in something totally new and unique in the field of entertainment," he commented. "We did it, in the knowledge that most of the people I talked to thought it would be a financial disaster—closed and forgotten within the first year."

Walt Disney was about to prove that "dreams really do come true."

"To all who come to this happy place—welcome!"

Sunday, July 17, 1955, dawned hot and sunny. Disneyland® Park would officially open to a curious world later in the morning. As the sun began to shine bright over the park, construction workers were still busy painting buildings and hoping that the recently packed asphalt on Main Street would cure in time.

During the months leading up to this momentous day, the construction of Disneyland had endured one of the wettest rainy seasons on record, a strike of the neighboring hot-asphalt plants, a plumber's strike, and the staff's collective anxiety over creating something totally new from scratch. Disneyland emerged from the orange groves of Anaheim in the short period between July 21, 1954, and July 17, 1955. In that time, the team responsible for making Disneyland a reality had grown from 21 employees and 5 consultants to 850 strong.

According to opening day statistics, Disneyland's construction had consumed over 2 million board feet of lumber, a million square feet of asphalt, and 5,000 cubic yards of poured concrete (seven times that amount of dirt had been moved to mold the berm that surrounded the park).

With all the construction and the pressure of last minute details, the original budget kept growing and growing. "I had different cost estimates; one time it was three and a half million and then I kept fooling around a little more with it and it got up to seven and a half million and I kept fooling around a little bit more and pretty soon it was twelve and a half and I think when we opened Disneyland it was seventeen million dollars," Walt once recalled.

At 10:00 A.M., the gates to Disneyland® Park officially opened for the first time. Six thousand invitations had been mailed to guests for the grand opening, but by the end of the day over 28,000 people had packed into the park. It was later discovered that because the opening of Disneyland was so anticipated, most of the tickets had been counterfeited.

In addition to the last minute construction headaches, the opening of the park was scheduled to be broadcast "live" on ABC-TV across the country to an estimated audience of 90 million viewers. Giant TV cameras and cables were scattered throughout the park, complicating the final opening preparations. In the infancy of television, a mere three cameras were

Children rush through Sleeping Beauty Castle on opening day (opposite page top).

The very first guests to enter the park on opening day—Kristine Vess and Michael Schwartner, ages five and seven—are welcomed by Walt Disney at the Main Entrance (above right).

The opening day parade marches down Main Street, U.S.A. during the live national television broadcast on ABC-TV (right). The broadcast was hosted by TV personality Art Linkletter, actor Bob Cummings, and an eventual president of the United States—Ronald Reagan.

Walt Disney and dignitaries gather in Town Square on Main Street, U.S.A. to rehearse the official dedication ceremonies of Disneyland (below).

California Governor Goodwin Knight and Fred Gurley, president of the Santa Fe Railroad, join Walt at the Main Street Station for the opening day festivities (opposite page top).

Walt and Governor Knight lead off the opening day parade in a vintage turn-of-the-century motorcar (opposite page bottom).

The opening day action in Town Square was broadcast live across America by ABC-TV, so that viewers could share the excitement (following pages).

normally used to cover a live event. The opening of Disneyland® Park incorporated 22 cameras to capture all the action.

As the TV crews prepared for the 4:30 P.M. broadcast, all was not well within the gates of the Magic Kingdom. Power went out on several attractions in Fantasyland, restaurants ran out of food and beverages, the *Mark Twain* steamboat took on water from overcrowding, and women were stepping out of their high-heeled shoes thanks to the still-soft asphalt on Main Street. And because of the plumber's strike, no drinking fountains were available throughout the day (the plumbers union had given Walt a choice between drinking fountains and restrooms).

Walt, however, was shielded from most of these disasters by the responsibilities of hosting the TV broadcast. With the help of TV stars Art Linkletter, Bob Cummings, and Ronald Reagan as co-hosts, Walt was busy running from locale to locale to dedicate each land during the live broadcast. The opening festivities featured such well-known Hollywood stars and dignitaries as Danny Thomas, Frank Sinatra, Sammy Davis, Jr., Irene Dunne, Fess Parker, Buddy Ebsen, the Mouseketeers, and Governor Goodwin Knight of California.

The live broadcast somewhat reflected the chaos occurring at the park, with numerous miscues and on-screen goofs. Walt missed his cue to read the dedication of Tomorrowland, Bob Cummings was caught kissing a young, pretty dancing girl in Frontierland, and during the opening parade Fess Parker (attired in his "Davy Crockett" buckskins) was introduced as

Cinderella. Nonetheless, the show was charming in its feeling of excitement and spontaneity.

The opening of Disneyland® Park would become famous in Disney lore and came to be known over the years as "Black Sunday." Despite bad reviews reflecting the opening day snafus, guests continued to flock to the park. "Disneyland is a work of love," stated Walt. "We didn't go into Disneyland with just the idea of making money." Walt's passion and love of the park was infectious and Disneyland welcomed its one millionth guest during the first seven weeks of operation.

As soon as Disneyland opened, Walt was already thinking ahead to how he could improve on the concept. "Disneyland will always be building and growing and adding new things," he promised. "New ways of having fun, of learning things and sharing the many exciting adventures which may be experienced here in the company of family and friends."

After almost 30 years of planning, Disneyland—"The Happiest Place on Earth"—was finally a reality and was on its way to becoming a beloved national treasure and an international institution. July 17, 1955 was just the beginning . . . .

A JOURNEY THROUGH DISNEYLAND

A journey through Disneyland® Park is a trip like no other. Here

in the original Magic Kingdom, you can literally walk in

Walt's footsteps, revisit adventures and attractions from

the past, and enjoy an ever-changing range of

new experiences. For first-time guests, Disneyland is a

big, shiny gift just waiting to be unwrapped, explored,

and enjoyed at every turn. For returning guests, a trip

to Disneyland is like visiting a dear friend or attending a family

reunion. Disneyland is a kaleidoscope of memories made anew.

So put on your Mickey Mouse ears, wind-up

your camera, and   get ready to explore "The

Happiest Place   on Earth—Disneyland!"

Disneyland® Park memories begin on Main Street, U.S.A. Time seems to slow and soften amid the smells of freshly baked muffins and candies, the steady clip-clop of the horse-drawn streetcar, and the twinkling pin lights outlining the gingerbread trim of the buildings. Through the years Main Street has become an unofficial hometown for the many Disneyland guests who have traversed its charming lane, experienced its unique shops, been entertained by its performers, and dined from its delightful menus.

"Here is America from 1890 to 1910, at the crossroads of an era," Walt Disney once commented. "Here the gas lamp is giving way to the electric lamp, and a newcomer, the sputtering 'horseless carriage,' has challenged Old Dobbin for the streetcar right-of-way." Inspired by Walt's own hometown of Marceline, Missouri, Main Street is the essence of the hometown America that greeted the dawn of the 20th century.

Town Square

Town Square is the civic center of this beguiling Victorian "hometown." The famed Disneyland Band gives daily concerts in the square, and would-be firefighters of the future can enjoy a playful trip into the past on Disneyland Fire Department No. 105. Above the firehouse Walt Disney kept a small apartment for his visits to Disneyland® Park. It is still maintained in Victorian-era décor and has remained virtually unchanged since Walt last used it back in the mid-1960s.

Town Square is also the hub of all Main Street transportation. From here guests can travel in style up Main Street in an open-air Horse-drawn Streetcar, Main Street Fire Engine (with clanging alarm bell), Horseless Carriage, or double-decker Omnibus.

BEHIND THE SCENES

Guests strolling down Main Street may notice that the ornate window advertisements above the attractions, stores, and restaurants add a nice, decorative element accentuating the turn-of-the-century theme. But only insiders are likely to know that most of the windows also serve a dual purpose of honoring Disneyland cast members, Imagineers, and artists who have left an indelible mark on Disneyland® Park. A good example is a window above the Emporium that reads: Elias Disney, Contractor, Est. 1895. Walt Disney's father was, in fact, a general contractor in the Midwest, who opened his contracting office in Chicago in 1895.

Disneyland Railroad

At the Main Street Station (right) guests can board one of the four authentic steam trains of the Disneyland Railroad for a grand circle tour of the park. The *C. K. Holliday* and *E. P. Ripley* were built from scratch at Walt Disney Studio in Burbank, California, prior to the opening of Disneyland® Park. The *Fred G. Gurley* was built in 1894 and was used in Louisiana to haul sugar cane. The *Ernest S. Marsh* was built in 1925 and was used at a lumber mill in New England. The four engines were named after the founders and executives of the Santa Fe Railroad.

During the trip around the park, guests travel along the rim of the Grand Canyon (below top) and journey through the incredible Primeval World (below bottom).

The Walt Disney Story

The Walt Disney Story Featuring Great Moments with Mr. Lincoln is an inspiring salute to Walt Disney, his pioneering career, and his respect and admiration for the wisdom and achievements of Abraham Lincoln. Located in the Main Street Opera House (below), the show features a display of Walt Disney's personal correspondence, early archival photos of the creation of Disneyland® Park, and replicas of Disney's two Studio offices, replete with authentic décor and personal memorabilia. Inside the office displays guests can see early plans for the Walt Disney World® Resort and ideas for future expansion in Disneyland, circa 1966.

The attraction also features an updated presentation of Great Moments with Mr. Lincoln, which first premiered at the 1964–65 New York World's Fair before coming to Disneyland. The show incorporates actual photographs from the Civil War and one of the most advanced examples of Audio-Animatronics® technology (above).

Sights, Sounds, and Smells

Main Street bustles with a variety of turn-of-the-century experiences for adventurous guests. You can sample homemade confections in the Candy Palace and Candy Kitchen (bottom right), thrill to the sounds of a melodious nickelodeon or enjoy some "flickers" via antique hand-cranked mutoscopes (inset, opposite page), catch a showing of Mickey Mouse in his landmark film *Steamboat Willie* (the first animated film with sound) at the Main Street Cinema, or have silhouettes created while you wait in the Silhouette Studio.

The Miracle of the Hub

One of the most innovative design elements of Disneyland® Park can be found at the end of Main Street, U.S.A. The park was planned with a central point of orientation—a "Plaza Hub"—where the entrances to all the "lands" converge, giving guests a convenient center from which to enter and exit. Within the park-like setting of the Plaza Hub, guests can sit among the colorful flowers and plot their next course through the Magic Kingdom or simply watch the world go by.

"Partners," a bronze statue of Walt Disney and Mickey Mouse, was unveiled in the center of the Plaza Hub in 1993. Set amidst a beautiful and ever-changing array of flowers, the impressive sculpture captures Walt and Mickey as they gaze down Main Street, U.S.A. The perfect focal point of the Hub—celebrating at one and the same time Disneyland's creator and its most famous icon—"Partners" has become one of the most photographed locations in the park.

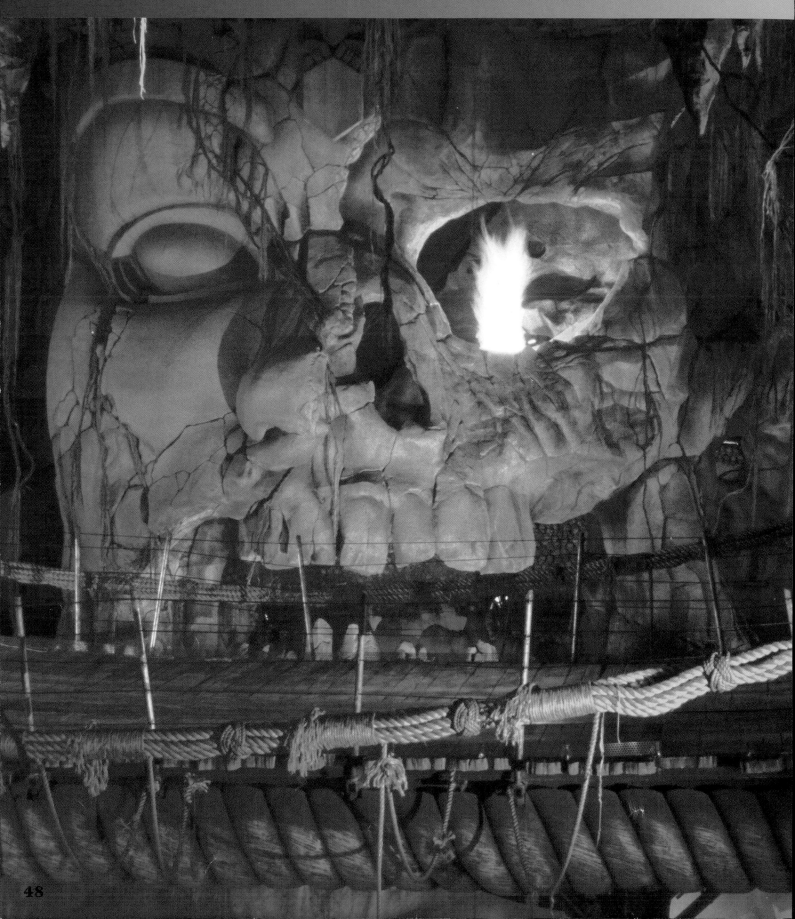

Guests encounter the wrath of the deity Mara inside the Temple of the Forbidden Eye as their transport vehicle speeds through the sinister catacombs and dangerous caverns of the Indiana Jones™ Adventure (opposite page).

Cool tranquil pools and cascading waterfalls are an escape from the tropical heat of Adventureland for some playful elephants along the waterways of the Jungle Cruise (right).

As brave Disneyland® Park guests enter Adventureland their senses are stirred by the sights of intense jungle foliage, the harrowing sounds of not-too-distant wild animals, and the aromas of tropical blossoms. In this remarkable realm of adventure and exploration guests experience an amazing amalgam of many of the world's far-off places and uncharted regions.

One quick turn can lead you to the hot sands of the Middle East (Aladdin's Oasis), the tropic splendor of Polynesia (Walt Disney's Enchanted Tiki Room), the vastness of Africa (Tarzan's Treehouse™), the exotic rivers of the world (Jungle Cruise), or the archeological ruins of Asia (Indiana Jones™ Adventure).

"Here is adventure," Walt Disney commented. "Here is romance. Here is mystery. Tropical rivers . . . silently flowing into the unknown. The unbelievable splendor of exotic flowers . . . the eerie sound of the jungle . . . with eyes that are always watching. This is Adventureland."

Indiana Jones™ and the Temple of the Forbidden Eye

Join Professor Jones deep inside Asia for the Indiana Jones™ Adventure. It's 1935 and discovery awaits in the Temple of the Forbidden Eye. Guests board well-worn troop transports that send them into a subterranean world where they have an unfortunate encounter with the mysterious temple deity Mara in the great Chamber of Destiny. Forced to flee, guests narrowly escape a collapsing bridge, booby traps, giant snakes, thousands of rats, and the prospect of being crushed by a 5-ton boulder. The Indiana Jones™ Adventure is one of the most technologically advanced attractions in any of the Disney theme parks. Each of the 16 troop transport vehicles has its own onboard ride control and audio system, allowing it to create nearly 160,000 journey combinations.

Jungle Cruise

One of the original attractions from the opening day of Disneyland® Park, the Jungle Cruise has hosted millions of would-be explorers aboard its dangerous (if you count the bad puns) excursions into the jungle. The Jungle Cruise replicates the environs of many of the world's most exotic rivers: the Irrawaddy River of Burma, Cambodia's Mekong, the Nile, the Congo River in Africa, and the Rapids of Kilimanjaro.

From the safety of their launches, guests can witness the gathering of animals on the African Veldt and experience the amazing sight of the "backside" of water under Schweitzer Falls (named after the famous explorer Dr. Albert Schweitzer). They may even catch a rare glimpse of the "Lost Safari," an unfortunate group of adventurers who always seem to be seen in the company of an angry rhino.

Enchanted Tiki Room

At the entrance to Adventureland, Walt Disney's Enchanted Tiki Room entertains guests with an irreverent presentation in which "the birdies sing and the flowers croon." The macaw hosts of the show—José, Michael, Fritz, and Pierre—have welcomed hundreds of thousands of guests into this special "world of joyous songs and wondrous miracles." During the show over 225 birds, flowers, and tikis delight the audience with a rousing rendition of "Let's All Sing Like the Birdies Sing."

Behind the Scenes

The opening of Walt Disney's Enchanted Tiki Room on June 23, 1963, marked the debut of a new era in Disneyland® Park attractions with the introduction of Audio-Animatronics®, an innovative electro-mechanical system that combines synchronized sound and movement to create three-dimensional animated figures. Since the show's premiere it has been a perennial favorite with park guests and its initial technology enabled the creation of more-elaborate Audio-Animatronics® shows such as Pirates of the Caribbean, Haunted Mansion, and Carousel of Progress.

Tarzan's Treehouse™

Tarzan's Treehouse™ celebrates the high-flying escapades of the "Lord of the Apes" 70 feet above Adventureland. Based on Disney's hit animated film *Tarzan*®, this new climb-through adventure allows guests to meet Tarzan, Jane, and the ferocious tiger Sabor. The tree itself is a very rare "species" known as a *Disneydendron semperflorens grandis* (meaning "large ever-blooming Disney tree"). It weighs 150 tons, features 450 branches and 6,000 leaves, and is anchored by massive "roots" reaching 42 feet into the ground.

Frontierland

A raft to Tom Sawyer Island, a Mike Fink Keel Boat, and the Columbia Sailing Ship bring to life the romance of river travel in Frontierland (opposite page).

The famed Golden Horseshoe Saloon has been providing rollicking music, song, and comedy to capacity audiences for over 45 years (right).

The breathtaking sight of the gleaming white Mark Twain Riverboat and the imposing gallantry of the Columbia Sailing Ship approaching the dock beckon guests into Frontierland, a robust panorama of America's pioneer past. As you pass through the stockade entrance you are surrounded by an amalgam of sights and sounds that authentically conjures up images from America's western expansion, from the bustling riverfronts of the Mississippi and Missouri Rivers of the late 1700s to the raucous and dusty desert southwest of the 1880s.

"Here we experience the story of our country's past . . . the colorful drama of Frontier America in the exciting days of the covered wagon and the stagecoach . . . the advent of the railroad . . . and the romantic riverboat," Walt Disney once commented. "Frontierland is a tribute to the faith, courage, and ingenuity of the pioneers who blazed the trails across America."

Frontierland

The heroes, legends, and tall tales of the American West live on in Frontierland. Here Davy Crockett is still "King of the Wild Frontier," Mike Fink is still "King of the River," Tom Sawyer eludes danger inside Injun Joe's Cave, Pecos Bill is still "the toughest critter west of the Alamo," and the ghostly legend of Big Thunder Mountain still haunts wary listeners.

Along the clapboard walkways, dusty trails, and rivers of Frontierland guests relive our rich pioneer heritage, including the charm of Old Mexico in Zocolo Park, an authentic encampment of Plains Indians along the riverbank, the rustic appeal of a chuckwagon meal served around a roaring campfire, and the rollicking entertainment inside the Golden Horseshoe saloon.

Rivers of America

The Rivers of America provides a variety of ways for would-be pioneers of all ages to explore the wilderness outposts of Frontierland. The dazzling white Mark Twain Riverboat carries guests upriver in southern elegance. When it opened in 1955, the *Mark Twain* was the first paddle wheeler built in the United States in half a century. The 84-foot tall, 10-gun Columbia Sailing Ship lets passengers relive life aboard an authentic replica of the first American ship to sail around the world. The *Columbia* was the first three-masted windjammer built in the United States in more than 100 years when it opened in 1958. Guests can get a close-up look of river life from one of the authentic Mike Fink Keel Boats as they navigate the backwaters of the Rivers of America.

Tom Sawyer Island

Walt Disney, who spent his early childhood in Missouri, personally oversaw the design of Tom Sawyer Island. Filled with such playful locales as Teeter-Totter Rock, Smuggler's Cove, and Tom and Huck's Treehouse the island is a cool, shady oasis of adventure. Young modern-day Tom Sawyers, Huck Finns, and Becky Thatchers still find fun in a high swaying suspension bridge, a rollicking barrel bridge, and the authenticity of log-hewn Fort Wilderness.

Big Thunder Mountain Railroad

Big Thunder Mountain Railroad—
"the wildest ride in the wilderness!"
—whisks brave guests back to the
Gold Rush era aboard runaway mine
trains that race around towering
buttes, dive into dangerous gulches,
and plunge deep into caverns filled
with bats and phosphorescent pools.
The reckless trains careen past raging
waterfalls, splash through still waters,
and finally encounter a deafening
earthquake from which the mountain
gets its name.

Disney Imagineers scouted
swap meets, auctions, ghost towns,
and abandoned mines throughout
the western United States for items
to incorporate into the theming of
the first incarnation of Big Thunder
Mountain Railroad. The attraction's
authentic mining props include a
1,200-pound cogwheel used to
break down ore, a hand-powered
drill press, and a 10-foot-tall 1880
mill stamp.

Dusk brings a special glow and glitter to the ornate balconies and pathways of New Orleans Square (opposite page).

Daylight shines brightly on this bend of the river, revealing intricate architectural details and providing a natural spotlight for the many flowers that grace New Orleans Square (right).

Here is the Paris of the American frontier: the Crescent City of New Orleans as it was 150 years ago. Within its sheltered courtyards and winding streets, elegance and charm mingle comfortably with the irreverent sounds of Dixieland jazz. In this romantic yet adventurous setting guests are immersed in the sights and sounds of New Orleans of the 1850s. The aromas of chicory and freshly baked fritters fill the air while the Louisiana state flag flies proudly overhead and the billowing white sails of a mighty galleon can be seen in the distance beyond the city.

New Orleans Square was added to Disneyland® Park in 1966. It was the first new "land" to be added to the park since its opening a decade before. From blossoming magnolia trees to intricate hand-painted murals, tiles, and mirrors, to authentic gas lamps and signage, the Disney Imagineers spared no detail in creating a port of elegance and adventure on this particular bend of the river.

Cajun Charm

Under the ornate wrought-iron balconies of New Orleans Square are found some of the most distinctive restaurants and shops in all of Disneyland® Park. Fine crystal and antique estate jewelry, hand-decorated parasols, rare high-end collectibles, and authentic Creole and Cajun spices and sauces can be found along the streets of New Orleans Square. At Café Orleans, the Royal Street Veranda, or the French Market, appetites can be satisfied with such temptations as spicy gumbo, sweet mint juleps, and mouth-watering fried chicken.

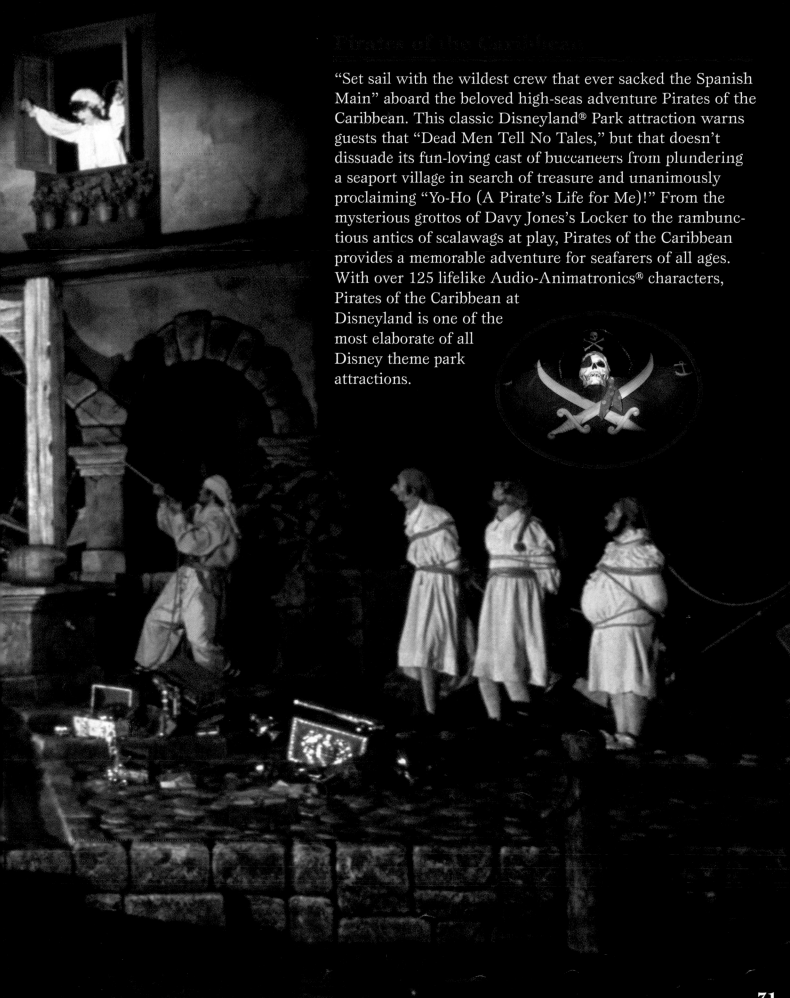

"Set sail with the wildest crew that ever sacked the Spanish Main" aboard the beloved high-seas adventure Pirates of the Caribbean. This classic Disneyland® Park attraction warns guests that "Dead Men Tell No Tales," but that doesn't dissuade its fun-loving cast of buccaneers from plundering a seaport village in search of treasure and unanimously proclaiming "Yo-Ho (A Pirate's Life for Me)!" From the mysterious grottos of Davy Jones's Locker to the rambunctious antics of scalawags at play, Pirates of the Caribbean provides a memorable adventure for seafarers of all ages. With over 125 lifelike Audio-Animatronics® characters, Pirates of the Caribbean at Disneyland is one of the most elaborate of all Disney theme park attractions.

The Haunted Mansion

"Welcome foolish mortals to the Haunted Mansion," home to 999 frightfully funny ghosts and happy haunts—but there is always room for one more! All the spirits are "just dying to meet you" as you tour this stately antebellum mansion in your own private "Doom Buggy," but beware of hitchhiking ghosts—they just may try to follow you home! The Haunted Mansion was in development for more than 10 years until its opening in 1969. The building exterior was actually completed in 1963, tantalizing guests for the next six years.

The organ located in the ballroom of the Mansion is the same organ played by Captain Nemo in Walt Disney's classic live-action film *20,000 Leagues Under the Sea*.

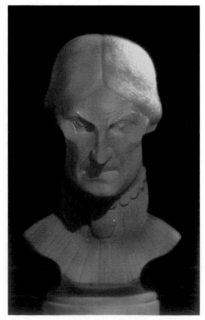

Critter Country

Intricate woodcarvings of Critter Country's signature trio—Brer Fox, Brer Bear, and Brer Rabbit—grace the shady queue area of Splash Mountain (opposite page).

Guests encounter a rustic signpost at the entrance to Critter Country that perfectly evokes its charm and hospitality (right).

Every day is a "Zip-a-Dee-Doo-Dah" kind of day in Critter Country, a little world of shady trees and cool streams tucked away in a quiet corner of the backwoods of Disneyland® Park. Nestled amid a forest of Aleppo, Canary Island, Monterey, and Italian stone pines, along with coast redwood, locusts, white birch, and evergreen elms, Critter Country is the perfect setting for long lazy afternoons and an opportunity to simply delight in the down-home country atmosphere. Keen eyes might spot wily Brer Rabbit outsmarting Brer Fox and Brer Bear atop Chickapin Hill. And keen ears will surely catch the applause and laughter drifting from the world-famous Country Bear Playhouse.

Guests with little cubs and hearty appetites can dine along the river's edge at the rustic Hungry Bear Restaurant or quench their thirst at the Brer Bar. And at the Briar Patch, under the looming shadow of Splash Mountain, guests can find items suitable to decorate any den, cave, or home.

The Country Bear Playhouse

The Country Bear Playhouse is home to a cast of bruins not seen in your typical national park. Nobody hibernates through the rollicking, foot-stomping, paw-pounding country-western musical antics of the bodacious Five Bear Rugs, the swinging Teddi Barra, and the sorrowful heart-tugging refrains of Big Al. Featuring more than 125 Audio-Animatronics® characters, the show changes seasonally with annual performances of The Country Bear Christmas Special and The Country Bear Vacation Hoedown.

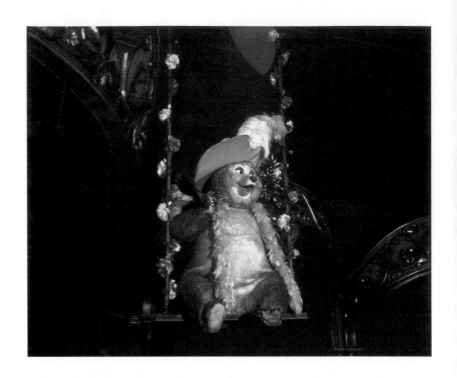

Davy Crockett's Explorer Canoes

Guests who want a hands-on experience of the frontier can hop aboard one of Davy Crockett's Explorer Canoes for an exciting paddle-powered excursion around the Rivers of America. Crashing through the wake of the mighty *Mark Twain* and encountering an authentic encampment of Plains Indians along the riverbank is only part of the adventure.

Inspired by Walt Disney's classic film *Song of the South* and the wise fables of Uncle Remus, Splash Mountain is the centerpiece of Critter Country and gives brave guests a chance to follow in the perilous footsteps of wily Brer Rabbit. Search for your "Laughing Place" as you journey through this exciting flume adventure which features five drops, including a hair-raising finale that sends you on a 52-foot, 45-degree-angle, 40-mph plunge into a watery briar patch below.

Fantasyland

Cross over the moat and through the archways of Sleeping Beauty Castle to enter "the happiest kingdom of them all"—Fantasyland. Enchanting tales of childhood adapted from Walt Disney's classic animated films come to life in this timeless realm of imagination. You can visit Never Land, soar through the skies with Dumbo, journey with little Alice to Wonderland, and travel the road to Pleasure Island with Pinocchio.

"Here is the world of imagination, hopes and dreams," Walt Disney stated on opening day. "In this timeless land of enchantment, the age of chivalry, magic, and make-believe are reborn—and fairy tales come true. Fantasyland is dedicated to the young and the young-in-heart—to those who believe that when you wish upon a star, your dreams come true."

Fantasyland Enchantment

Dusk casts a veil of additional magic over this happy land of childhood. The medieval splendor of Sleeping Beauty Castle is complemented by the deep shadows of the mighty snowcapped Matterhorn in the distance. Walt Disney once said that "Fantasy, if it's really convincing, can't become dated, for the simple reason that it represents a flight into a dimension that lies beyond the reach of time . . . and nobody gets any older."

King Arthur Carrousel

Beckoning guests through the archway of Sleeping Beauty Castle is the glittering sight of King Arthur Carrousel. The horses of the carrousel are 90 to 110 years old and are hand-carved and hand-painted classics—no two are exactly alike. The turntable for the carrousel was made around 1875 and came from Canada. Most of the 19th-century horses were hand-carved in Germany.

Sleeping Beauty Castle has stood guard over Fantasyland since 1955. The pinks and the blues of the regal, Bavarian-style castle are a nod to the princess for whom the castle is named. Sharp-eyed guests will notice such details as Walt Disney's family crest above the castle entrance and actual 22-karat gold leafing adorning the spires.

Alice in Wonderland

Don't be late for a very important date! Climb aboard your very own private Caterpillar and journey down the rabbit hole to join Alice in her marvelous adventures in Wonderland. Unique to Disneyland® Park, the Alice in Wonderland adventure is filled with such memorable scenes as the Unbirthday Party, Tweedle Dum and Tweedle Dee, the Garden of Flowers, the March of the Cards, and a fateful round of croquet with the ever-explosive Queen of Hearts.

Pinocchio's Daring Journey

Pinocchio's Daring Journey premiered in Fantasyland in 1983. Guests are sure to be captivated by the lonely woodcarver Geppetto and his desire to have a real son. Along cobblestone alpine roads, guests follow little Pinocchio and his faithful conscience Jiminy Cricket as they attempt to avoid fateful encounters with the conniving Foulfellow and Gideon, the villainous puppeteer Stromboli, and Monstro the Whale. With the "wishing star" as their guide, guests meet the lovely Blue Fairy and ultimately share in Pinocchio's happy ending.

Casey Jr. Circus Train

Guests aboard the Casey Jr. Circus Train (secure in their various cages, boxcars, and cabooses) will cheer along as Casey proclaims "I think I can, I think I can, I think I can" while he chugs and puffs his way through the hills and valleys of Storybook Land. Casey Jr. Circus Train is based upon the brave little circus train featured in Walt Disney's beloved animated film *Dumbo*.

Storybook Land Canal Boats

Aboard the Storybook Land Canal Boats, guests glide past miniature homes and settings from some of Disney's most adored characters and animated films including Geppetto's Village, the Dwarfs' Diamond Mine, and Aladdin's city of Agrabah. Created at 1/12th scale, the intricately detailed dwellings are complemented by actual living miniature shrubs, flowers, and trees including 150-year-old miniature pine trees.

Mad Tea Party

Guests can spin and spin and spin their cup and saucer in any direction in the Mad Tea Party, a life-size Unbirthday Party. With colorful Chinese paper lanterns hanging overhead and the familiar strains of the "Unbirthday Song" in the air, guests will surely feel as if they stepped right into the beloved storybook or Disney film of Alice in Wonderland.

Dumbo the Flying Elephant

Soar high over Fantasyland aboard Dumbo the Flying Elephant, a tribute to the world's most famous flying pachyderm. A well-known European manufacturer of circus organs built the attraction's vintage mechanical band organ. Constructed around 1915, the organ weighs three-quarters of a ton and its circus-like music can be heard over a mile away.

Peter Pan's Flight

On Peter Pan's Flight guests pilot their own pirate galleon, sailing through the nursery of the Darling family (the toy alphabet blocks in the nursery spell the word "Disney" from the bottom up), gliding over London, and following Tinker Bell towards the "Second Star to the Right" and straight on to Never Land. Amid twinkling stars, you can look down and spy such Never Land locales as Mermaid Lagoon and Skull Rock. More than half of the approximately 350 miles of fiber optics used throughout Fantasyland appear in Peter Pan's Flight.

Snow White's Scary Adventures

Enter a timeless tale of romance in Snow White's Scary Adventures. The lovable Seven Dwarfs celebrate with a "Silly Song" while the evil Queen disguises herself as an old peddler woman to tempt Snow White with a juicy cursed apple. Although the Queen often can be seen staring out of a window above Snow White's Scary Adventures, everyone lives happily ever after with the arrival of the Prince and love's first kiss.

Mr. Toad's Wild Ride

Madcap adventurer J. Thaddeus Toad welcomes guests inside stately Toad Hall as he test drives his all-new motorcar and takes everyone on a wild ride across the English countryside to "Nowhere in Particular." Along the way guests race, leap, and crash their way through Mr. Toad's trials and tribulations inside one of Fantasyland's most beloved attractions. The coat of arms for J. Thaddeus Toad, featured in the décor of Toad Hall, is emblazoned with the motto Toadi Acceleratio Semper Absurda ("Speeding with Toad is always absurd").

Snow White Wishing Well

Site of numerous wedding proposals, the Snow White Wishing Well and Grotto provides a tranquil and romantic setting along the east side of the Sleeping Beauty Castle moat. The marble figures of Snow White and the Seven Dwarfs were a gift to Walt Disney from an Italian sculptor. Sharp-eared guests can hear Snow White's hopeful refrain of "I'm Wishing" echoing in the depths of the well.

Triton Gardens & Ariel's Grotto

Under the shadow of the mighty Matterhorn is Triton Gardens, where fanciful spouts of water dance and leap across the walkway to the delight of guests. Across the way, little Ariel poses for pictures with guests in her impressive clamshell setting.

The Sword in the Stone

Every day little would-be monarchs can follow in the footsteps of young King Arthur as they try to remove the legendary sword Excalibur from its anvil and stone resting-place. With a little help from bumbling Merlin the Wizard, royal hopefuls sometimes successfully budge the sword and become rulers of the realm for the day.

Matterhorn Bobsleds

The Matterhorn Bobsleds had its origin in the 1959 Disney film *The Third Man on the Mountain.* Towering 14 stories above Fantasyland, the snow-capped Matterhorn (a 1/100th scale replica of its Swiss namesake) is the setting for a thrilling race through ominous ice caves and a frightening chance encounter with the Abominable Snowman. Along its icy slopes are thundering waterfalls, alpine forests, and tranquil ponds. The camp of the lost climbing expedition inside the Matterhorn is a tribute to former Walt Disney Company President Frank G. Wells. Prior to his passing in 1994, Wells had climbed the highest mountains on six of the seven continents.

"it's a small world"

Guests have been captivated by "it's a small world" since its premiere at Disneyland® Park in 1966. A salute to the children of the world, this delightful attraction speaks the international language of goodwill. Its impressive exterior, featuring spires and finials covered in 22-karat-gold leafing, playfully represents world landmarks, including France's Eiffel Tower, Italy's Leaning Tower of Pisa, and India's famed Taj Mahal. Aboard their boats, guests journey beyond the Topiary Garden and drift with the tide into "The Happiest Cruise That Ever Sailed."

During the winter, the attraction is transformed into the spectacular "it's a small world" Holiday, in which the holiday traditions of many nations are fancifully displayed and the attraction's famous score is beautifully integrated with such holiday favorites as "Deck the Halls" and "Jingle Bells."

Bursting with color and frenetic energy, Mickey's Toontown is a 1930s classic Disney cartoon come to wacky "reel" life. Here in this social hub of "Toon" life, animated stars such as Mickey Mouse, Minnie Mouse, Donald Duck, Goofy, Chip 'n Dale, and Roger Rabbit live, work, and play, much to the delight of guests of all ages.

Toontown legend has it that Mickey Mouse founded the three-acre community in the 1930s as a retreat from the bustle of Hollywood. Until its opening in 1993 Toontown was kept secret, the only human allowed being Walt Disney. Mickey suggested in the early 1950s that the vacant property to the south be turned into Disneyland® Park. Thirty-eight years later, Mickey decided to open Toontown to the public.

Signage leading into Mickey's Toontown denotes such organizations as the DAR (Daughters of the Animated Reel), Loyal Knights of the Inkwell, Optimist Intoonational, and the Benevolent and Protective Order of Mouse.

"Toon" in to Toontown

The municipality of Mickey's Toontown is divided into three areas: to the east is the ever active Downtown, in the west are the tranquil environs of Mickey's Neighborhood (home to Mickey, Minnie, Goofy, Donald, and Chip 'n Dale), and Toontown Square is situated in the middle. Mickey's Toontown features some of the most unique architecture in Disneyland® Park, with no straight lines, right angles, or conventional methods of construction to be found. Here mailboxes and manhole covers have personalities (and voices) all their own.

Goofy's Bounce House

Inside Goofy's Bounce House kids can literally bounce right off the walls of this wacky home. The floor has just a little extra "cush" and the sofa is so fluffy that it can give little guests a lift! After seeing the instability of the inside, you can easily understand why from the outside Goofy's Bounce House looks like it just might bounce off its foundation.

Gadget's Go-Coaster

Gadget's Go-Coaster, located next to Donald's Boat on Toon Lake, is a high-speed, splash-down contraption for children of all ages. Guests travel in vehicles that resemble oversized acorns. Appearing to be made from large spools, springs, rubber bands, toothbrushes, combs, and other assorted household goods, this little coaster is sure to give guests to Mickey's Toontown a beautiful view along with a few butterflies in their stomachs.

Mickey's House and Meet Mickey

The welcome mat is always out for guests to Mickey's House and Meet Mickey. Inside Mickey's California bungalow home guests can see where Mickey unwinds and view mementos of his famed career.

Through the backyard guests can tour Mickey's Movie Barn Sound Stage where he keeps many of the props from some of his most famous film roles. In the Movie Barn guests can drop in to say hello and pose with Mickey as he works on a new film project.

Minnie's House

Painted in romantic hues of lavender and pink, Minnie's House is situated cozily right next door to Mickey's. Inside Minnie's House, guests can play with her computerized vanity, bang out a tune on her pots and pans in the kitchen, or assist her with baking a cake for Mickey. Outside guests can see her colorful garden and make a wish in her charming wishing well.

Donald's Boat

Walk across the gangplank over Toon Lake and aboard Donald's Boat—the *Miss Daisy.* Home to the irascible yet lovable Donald Duck, the charming boat gives little sailors the opportunity to clang bells and blow whistles. The *Miss Daisy,* named for Donald's sweetheart Daisy, also provides a spectacular view of Mickey's Neighborhood and the Downtown area of Mickey's Toontown.

Chip 'n Dale's Treehouse

The Toontown home of Chip 'n Dale, Donald Duck's mischievous chipmunk adversaries, is fittingly nestled in a colorful acorn tree. Here little guests can meet Chip 'n Dale and explore their treetop home.

Jolly Trolley

The bright red and gold-trimmed Jolly Trolley rambles through all of Mickey's Toontown, winding around Roger Rabbit's fountain in Downtown Toontown, traveling into Mickey's Neighborhood, and circling Mickey's fountain. A large gold wind-up key on top of the engine turns as the trolley runs. Disney Imagineers fitted the Jolly Trolley with a Tooned-up chassis and various wheel sizes to produce its ambling, undulating cartoonlike gait.

Roger Rabbit's Car Toon Spin

Ride along with Lenny the Cab in Roger Rabbit's Car Toon Spin, in which Roger tries to save his lovely Jessica from the dastardly Weasels and a fateful plunge in the dreaded "Dip." On this twirling and whirling adventure, go on a wacky trip through cartoon back alleys in a quest to save Jessica and all the citizens of Toontown. The attraction contains 16 Audio-Animatronics® figures, 59 animated props, and 20 special effects.

Tomorrowland

The Astro Orbiter, the signature attraction of Tomorrowland (opposite page), is a colorful background for the high-speed Rocket Rods.

The towering Astro Orbiter stands as a welcoming beacon in Tomorrowland (right).

As guests cross over into Tomorrowland they embark on an exciting journey into "Imagination and Beyond." This intriguing realm of imagination, discovery, and wonder was inspired by such classic futurists as Jules Verne, H. G. Wells, and Leonardo da Vinci, along with modern visionaries like George Lucas. In 1955 when the original Tomorrowland opened, Walt Disney described it as "A vista into a world of wondrous ideas, signifying man's achievements . . . a step into the future, with predictions of constructive things to come. Tomorrow offers new frontiers in science, adventure, and ideals: the Atomic Age . . . the challenge of outer space . . . and the hope for a peaceful and unified world."

Today Tomorrowland, with its whirling spaceships, zooming rocket vehicles, lush vegetation, and kinetic sculptures and fountains, builds upon Walt Disney's original vision and presents an exciting look beyond the stars to a future full of promise and hope.

Aboard the Astro Orbiter, guests pilot their own spaceships through a fantastic animated "astronomical model" of planets and constellations. Its colorful rockets circling a series of moving planets, the Astro Orbiter is a radiant and impressive cosmos of colors in tones of burnished copper and brass. The Astro Orbiter welcomes guests at the entrance to Tomorrowland and, both day and night, is an impressive futuristic backdrop to their visits.

Honey, I Shrunk the Audience

Honey, I Shrunk the Audience is a hilarious 3-D film experience that gives guests to the Imagination Institute a change of perspective. Join noted Professor Wayne Szalinski as he is honored as the "Inventor of the Year." But things get a little out of control and the audience is ultimately "shrunk" by one of Szalinski's inventions.

Disneyland Monorail

The Disneyland® Monorail, designated "a National Historic Mechanical Engineering Landmark," was the very first daily operating monorail in the Western Hemisphere when it opened in 1959. Since then it has transported thousands of guests along its 2.4-mile "highway in the sky," providing round-trip transportation from the high-tech world of Tomorrowland to the comfort of the Disneyland Resort hotels.

Innoventions

Innoventions is a two-level interactive pavilion that brings near-future high-technology into the world of today. Innoventions features products and concepts from the world's leading industries, and is divided into five main technology sections: Sports/Recreation, Home, Entertainment, Workplace, and Transportation. After enjoying the interactive first half of the attraction, guests flow to a center atrium where they ascend to the upper-level concept presentations, all clustered around an impressive illuminated tree that is literally "wired" for the future.

BEHIND THE SCENES

Tomorrowland's landmark Carousel Theater, home to Innoventions, previously housed the fondly remembered attractions Carousel of Progress and America Sings. As a tribute to the original Carousel of Progress attraction, its popular theme song, "There's a Great Big Beautiful Tomorrow," has been updated and is featured as the theme song for Innoventions.

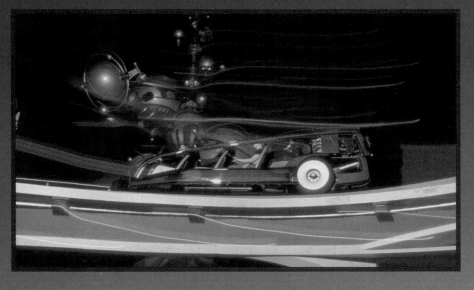

Rocket Rods

With screeching tires and turbo-charged engine growls, the Rocket Rods (the fastest attraction in Disneyland® Park) race above, through, and around the landscape of Tomorrowland. Aboard this thrilling journey guests test-drive high-speed vehicles of the future along an elevated highway above Tomorrowland. Prior to boarding, guests are completely surrounded by nine movie screens which feature footage of Walt Disney presenting glimpses of transportation vehicles from the past and future.

Observatron

Soaring above Tomorrowland is Observatron, a colorful, highly kinetic sculpture representing the imaginative world of tomorrow and beyond. Sitting impressively atop the Rocket Rods loading platform, Observatron signals the quarter hour with an impressive array of movements, lights, and vibrant music. Under Observatron is the official Disneyland® Park home of Radio Disney. Through soundproof glass, guests can see into Radio Disney's state-of-the-art radio studio and watch daily live broadcasts carried across the nation on "the radio network just for kids."

Space Mountain

Under its metallic spires of green and copper, Space Mountain hosts a thrilling, high-speed adventure through deep space. An energetic and heart-pounding onboard soundtrack blasts in the background as guests on this out-of-this-world journey are whisked through the darkness of outer space, past giant meteors and shooting stars, and eventually returned after a hair-raising re-entry to the spaceport.

Star Tours

Inside Star Tours, a bustling inter-galactic travel agency leads guests to a spaceport where they quickly board a StarSpeeder 3000 for a perilous journey to the moon of Endor. Based on George Lucas's famed film series, Star Tours takes its passengers on a harrowing trip through the cosmos, guided by Rex (a rookie pilot), R2D2, and C3PO. Along the way passengers brave a wild trip through comets, narrowly escape an intergalactic dogfight, and successfully maneuver through the dangerous chasms of a Death Star.

BEHIND THE SCENES

In the Star Tours queue area guests can hear the announcement: "Mr. Egroeg Sacul, please see the Star Tours agent at gate number 3." Egroeg Sacul is George Lucas spelled backward.

Cosmic Waves, an impressive interactive ring of fountains in Tomorrowland, is a vertical liquid landscape that shoots upward towards the stars in an unpredictable fashion. Within the ring of fountains is a black granite ball, weighing nearly 2 tons, which appears to be floating on a spray of water. In the evening, Cosmic Waves comes alive with color as the gyrating fountains are lit from below in a constantly changing stream of color.

The Moonliner stood in Tomorrowland as a landmark on opening day, July 17, 1955. The Rocket to the Moon attraction, of which it was a part, didn't open, however, until a week later. The Moonliner became the Douglas Moonliner in 1962. It vanished from the Tomorrowland landscape in 1967, but the attraction remained, updated to Flight to the Moon. The attraction became Mission to Mars in 1975. Today, the Moonliner is back, once again acting as a landmark, towering over the new Tomorrowland panorama.

BACKSTAGE ADVENTURES IN THE MAGIC KINGDOM

At Disneyland® Park, producing happiness for millions of guests from around the world is a full-time job—365  days a year, 24 hours a day. However, a great deal of the work that guarantees smiles in the park occurs

"backstage," away from the guests. There are many important cast members whose role is to prepare the Disneyland show for the next day, insuring that the cast is well-groomed, trained, and properly costumed, that the stage is set and ready, and that everything receives just the right amount of pixie dust.

The Language of Disneyland

The Disney University at Disneyland® Park established new methods of recruitment and training. Applying the terminology of show business to modern training applications, the Disney University philosophy promotes Disneyland as a large outdoor show, where every staff member plays an important role, regardless of his or her position or title.

A special language and set of principles continue to form the bedrock of all the Disney theme parks:

- ❱ Disneyland doesn't have customers—it *plays host to guests.*
- ❱ The park doesn't cater to crowds—it *entertains an audience.*
- ❱ There are no employees; instead there are Disneyland *cast members* whose role is to create happiness for park guests.
- ❱ Cast members at Disneyland wear *costumes from wardrobe* instead of uniforms.
- ❱ Disneyland is not an amusement park—with its creation the term *theme park* came into use.
- ❱ Unlike a standard amusement park or carnival, which features rides, Disneyland has more than 60 *adventures* and *attractions.*
- ❱ Cast members work *onstage* or *backstage.*

One Disney University practice that has caught on with many companies is the use of nametags and the implementation of a first-name policy. At Disneyland the only "Mr." is Mr. Toad. According to a 1955 orientation handbook, Disneyland operates "on a first-name basis. We go about our work in a businesslike way, but we feel that work can be fun, and that we can all be friendly and cheerful while we are doing the things we are assigned to do."

Another guiding principle of the Disney University is the application of "The Disneyland Look." In planning the costumes for Disneyland® Park, designers are careful to ensure that each costume properly and seamlessly themes to each land or attraction. It is imperative that the cast members and their costumes add to, and not detract from, the overall show.

Walt Disney realized that the neat and well-groomed appearance of cast members would be an essential part of the overall guest experience. He didn't want modern-day society encroaching on the fantasy of Disneyland through the display of contemporary trends in fashion and grooming.

The training philosophy of Disney University has always placed an emphasis on casting the right people in the right roles. "You can dream, create, design, and build the most wonderful place in the world . . . but it requires people to make the dream a reality," Walt once remarked.

The Disneyland traditions taught at the Disney University—such as the principles of guest hospitality, service, and guest satisfaction, along with "The Disneyland Look," the language of Disneyland, and the first-name policy—have become universal trademarks of the park. Over the past 45 years, more than 400,000 Disneyland cast members have graduated from the Disney University and have upheld its traditions and principles in their continuing Disney careers or have implemented them in new careers in outside fields and professions.

The Disney University at Disneyland provides ongoing cast-member training and enrichment for the entire Disneyland Resort, including orientation, management classes, and career counseling. It was the prototype for the successful training programs now in effect at the other Disney theme parks and resorts around the world (opposite page).

The neat and well-groomed "Disneyland Look" has kept the Disneyland "show" fresh over the past four decades (below).

Landscaping with Character

When guests walk through the Main Entrance of Disneyland® Park they come face-to-face with a Magic Kingdom landscape landmark—the bright and colorful floral image of Mickey's smiling face below the Main Street Station. Perhaps one of the most photographed images on earth during the past 45 years, the icon, which is replanted nine times per year, is a fine example of the remarkable landscape architecture found throughout the park.

Located within the eight themed lands of Disneyland are more than 800 species of plants, representing more than 40 nations around the world. The variety of plants and landscaping techniques utilized within the park, including about 5,000 trees and 40,000 shrubs, makes Disneyland one of the most extensive and diverse botanical locales in the western United States. The landscape panorama of the park includes lush jungles, dense forests, beautiful gardens, manicured lawns, lazy rivers, and tranquil ponds.

The Disneyland landscape wasn't always so perfect. Prior to opening day, Disneyland landscapers raided nurseries from San Diego to Santa Barbara in an attempt to gather enough plants and trees to finish the landscaping on time and on budget. "I remember when we opened . . . we didn't have enough money to finish the landscaping and I had Bill Evans

The "Mickey Planter" at the Disneyland Main Entrance greets guests as they begin their day at the park. The planter and Main Street Train Station are two of the park's most recognizable images (opposite page).

Vast varieties of plants, shrubs, and trees are cultivated backstage behind the park where they await their "cue" to appear onstage (below).

Pruning and replanting are never-ending chores within the Magic Kingdom. Countless flowerbeds need regular care, and fanciful topiaries require frequent trims (above and below).

In Tomorrowland, the landscaping is good enough to eat—lemon and orange trees, along with lettuce and cabbage, greet guests at the base of the Astro Orbiter (opposite page).

[the chief landscape director for Disneyland] go out and put Latin tags on all the weeds," Walt Disney once jokingly recalled.

Today, however, Disneyland® Park is a horticulturist's dream come true. Supervising the planting of over 1 million annuals every year, along with 25 varieties of grasses covering more than 5 acres, the 60-person Disneyland landscaping team keeps the Magic Kingdom blooming year round. To help maintain the landscaping in peak form, a water-saving computer system regulates the water usage of more than 50,000 drip emitters and sprinkler heads throughout the park.

Although virtually all the trees, flowers, and shrubs that make up the Disneyland landscape were imported, there is one group of trees native to Disneyland. The giant eucalyptus trees that sprout from behind City Hall in Town Square on Main Street, U.S.A. have stood in the same place since the early 1900s. They act as background foliage for both Adventureland and Main Street, but the trees were initially planted to serve as a windbreak for the orange groves that originally stood on the property.

One of the newer and more unique landscaping projects recently undertaken at Disneyland has been the introduction of an "agrifuture" to Tomorrowland. Nearly every landscape element in Tomorrowland is now edible, in what has been called "The World's Most Unusual Edible Landscape." Most of the trees are fruit bearing, such as orange, apple, lemon, lime, banana, and persimmon. Other edible trees dotting the

A playful topiary elephant stands guard near Dumbo the Flying Elephant in Fantasyland (right).

Gardeners need to take special care when attending to the intricate and complicated landscaping needs of Storybook Land (below).

landscape include olive, date palm, pecan, fig, pomegranate, and avocado. The shrubs and ground covers are also edible, with the plantings changing seasonally.

Those would-be horticulturists who prefer their plants to teem with a little more personality and character need look no further than Fantasyland. Frolicking beneath the pastel spires of the "it's a small world" attraction is an assemblage of fanciful topiary characters made famous at Disneyland® Park in the early 1960s.

Topiaries, which come in all shapes and sizes, take three to five years of constant care to create. Other topiary examples in the park include a pyramid of pachyderms near Dumbo the Flying Elephant and a beautiful swan gliding across a bed of deep blue flowers in front of Sleeping Beauty Castle.

The lengths to which Disney landscapers will go to meet their goals can perhaps best be seen along the banks and hills of the Storybook Land Canal Boats and Casey Jr. Circus Train. To complement the tiny houses and villages found within these two attractions, Disney landscapers' attention to detail extended all the way down to the smallest tree in the park—a 1-foot dwarf spruce. All the landscaping found within the attractions must conform to the required 1/12th scale, making it one of the more tricky gardening jobs in the park.

Aside from enhancing a beautiful environment, the landscaping at Disneyland also serves another purpose: to separate Disneyland from the distractions of the outside world. This is achieved through the heavily planted 15-foot-high earthen berm that surrounds the park.

Costuming a Cast of Thousands

To effectively play their respective roles in the Disneyland® Park show, cast members must be outfitted in appropriate costumes. Over the years the imagination and creativity of the designers, buyers, seamstresses, coordinators, and administrators who work in the Disneyland Costume Division have touched virtually every onstage Disneyland cast member.

The skill and expertise of the 350 professionals who make up the Disneyland Costume Division have been recognized by their counterparts at the other Disney theme parks around the world. The Costume Division has not only successfully costumed the cast members of the Disneyland Resort, but has also designed and created costumes for the Magic Kingdom® Park at Walt Disney World® Resort, Epcot®, Disney-MGM Studios, Tokyo Disneyland, and Disneyland Paris.

The costumes created for Disneyland can be as casual and comfortable as those worn by the Disneyland parking lot hosts and hostesses to the elaborate attire of the parade and show performers. Costumes play a very important role in communicating the various themes and time periods represented throughout Disneyland, so visual authenticity is a primary design concern for the Costume Division.

From initial design to use in the park, a new costume requires 37 steps and six to eight months to produce. It takes a collaborative team effort between designers, Imagineers, operations managers, color consultants, seamstresses, cutters, tailors, and workroom personnel to successfully create just one costume. Special considerations must be given to the exact use of the costume: is it for entertainment purposes or an actual, functional outfit? This will determine which fabrics are chosen, as well as influence design considerations affecting the costume's comfort and practicality.

The cast member costumes of Disneyland take many forms and styles such as these examples from Pirates of the Caribbean (above top), Circle D Corral (above middle), and The Golden Horseshoe (above bottom). Disneyland Costuming provides costumes for cast members who work onstage in the park as well as certain roles backstage such as maintenance, facilities, and landscaping. Thousands of reams of fabric and countless spools of yarn and threads are used annually (left).

The life of an average attraction costume is about nine months. Cast members are issued a clean costume at the beginning of their day and return it to costuming at the end of their shift. The costumes are created according to varying sizes and are thoroughly inspected, repaired (if needed), and cleaned every evening. During the peak summer season, over 65,000 costume garments are exchanged per week for cleaning. Each year, approximately 100,000 individual items are repaired and 150,000 costumes replaced.

With a total of 14,000 cast members to outfit during peak season, the Costume Division features an inventory of over 800,000 pieces, along with a warehouse containing over one million yards of fabric in 1,200 distinct styles. Additionally, the Costume Division is responsible for all costumes used by the more than 1,100 Audio-Animatronics® cast members in Disneyland, including the period costumes found in the Haunted Mansion and the charming international costumes of "it's a small world."

Not surprisingly, there is one little personality who has his very own extensive wardrobe at Disneyland® Park. Mickey Mouse has a costume and special outfit for practically every occasion—from his California surf attire to his formal top hat and tails. Although Disneyland guests recognize him best in his familiar long red pants, tail coat, and bow tie, Mickey can be seen throughout the day in several different costumes. During his evening appearances in the nighttime spectacular Fantasmic!, Mickey dons both his black and white outfit from his hit animated film *Steamboat Willie* (1928) and his famed Sorcerer's Apprentice robe and hat from *Fantasia* (1940).

A team of costume designers brings their unique sense of style to the fashions of Disneyland (above top), while just the right fabrics are chosen for showmanship and durability (above middle). In the Costume Division seamstress shops, prototype costumes are created to check for flexibility of wear and accuracy of theming (above bottom). The Costume Division also provides the very latest in fashions for the many princesses of Disneyland, yet there are certain styles that are just timeless—and recognizable (right).

After completing their shift on one of the Main Street Horse-drawn Streetcars some of the fine Disneyland draft horses are led back to their home at the Circle D Corral (left). The four-legged cast members of the Circle D Corral are groomed, exercised, and fed daily in a setting reminiscent of a working ranch of 100 years ago, except with all the modern amenities (below).

Down at the Circle D Corral

The Circle D Corral is a picturesque and quiet spot nestled in the backstage area of Disneyland® Park, just beyond the berm and northern border of Frontierland. There, under the tall shady trees that serve as the forest backdrop of Frontierland, sits a little farmhouse. Once home to one of the original landowners who worked a small strawberry field on the site, the little farmhouse is now the office and animal care center of the Circle D Corral.

Established during the early days of the park and originally known as the Pony Farm, the Circle D Corral is home to the various animals that work at Disneyland. The most often-seen residents are the award-winning horses, including the mighty French Percherons, Belgians, and the English Clydesdales that pull the Main Street, U.S.A. horse-drawn trolleys, along with various carriages and parade wagons. The largest horse at the Circle D Corral is Duke, a Percheron draft horse weighing more than 2,400 pounds. The horses work four days a week, four hours per day.

The Circle D Corral features its own blacksmith shop and an impressive collection of personalized and distinctive harnesses created on a vintage 1911 sewing machine. Today the personalized harnesses are made for Disneyland by a well-known Canadian harnessmaker.

Other livestock at the ranch include an assortment of ornery mules, playful goats, sheep, ducks, and free-roaming chickens. The Circle D Corral is also responsible for the homing pigeons used in various special events at the park along with the graceful swans that call the moat of Sleeping Beauty Castle home.

Remarkably, although situated in the middle of the ever-busy backstage area of Disneyland, the Circle D Corral provides a tranquil setting. Because of the surrounding aspen, pine, and oak trees, the Circle D Corral experiences changing seasons—an unusual occurrence in Southern California.

For all the peaceful atmosphere, the Circle D Corral is a truly functional ranch with all the requirements, chores, and responsibilities of the real thing. The sign above the barn says it all—"Home of the Happiest Horses on Earth."

Behind the Scenes Magic

From the moment guests walk into Disneyland® Park they encounter a little Disney magic at every turn. Whether it's delighting in the antics of the lovable Disney characters, watching fireworks burst over Sleeping Beauty Castle, or watching Main Street, U.S.A. illuminate with light at dusk, Disneyland is filled with bits of enchantment.

Not surprisingly, it takes more than a little Disney magic to keep the show going successfully 365 days a year at the high standards that have become a hallmark of Disneyland. To maintain Disneyland on a daily basis, a staff of over 600 cast members are responsible for keeping the park clean and in top operational shape.

The philosophy of maintaining an impeccably clean park dates back to Walt Disney himself. "If you keep a place clean, people will respect it . . . it's like any other show on the road; it must be kept clean and fresh." During any given day at Disneyland, guests can see a team of Custodial Guest Services cast members enforcing this philosophy as they swarm over various areas of the park, with brooms in hand, making sure everything is as tidy as possible.

After the park closes, another team of Custodial Guest Services cast members descends on the park to get it ready for another day. Throughout the night dedicated cast members steam-clean the streets and pathways, buff the brass poles of the Carrousel, shine windows, vacuum and shampoo carpets, dust shelves, polish and wax floors, wash and clean all attraction queue areas, and scrub all kitchens and restrooms.

The efficient cast members of Disneyland Custodial Guest Services utilize over 1,000 brooms, 500 dustpans, and 3,000 mops per year to keep the park clean. Their successful efforts are all the more amazing when, on average, approximately 30 tons of trash is collected at Disneyland on a busy day, resulting in the collection of 12 million pounds a year.

With the adoption of "Environmentality," Disneyland® Park has taken Walt's philosophy of cleanliness one step further. This extensive recycling program is responsible for the yearly reprocessing of 2.4 million pounds of cardboard, 512,000 pounds of office paper, and 6,550 pounds of aluminum cans.

Meanwhile, the Disneyland Facilities and Maintenance teams work around the clock to insure that Disneyland is running smoothly. Their work is probably the most transparent, yet most vital, to the daily operation of Disneyland. Everything from the correct time on the clock tower of the Main Street Train Station to the right number of acorns in Chip 'n Dale's Treehouse, and everything in between, is the responsibility of these two teams.

One of the most important tasks of the Facilities and Maintenance teams is to nightly inspect the tracks and ride vehicles of the various adventures and attractions in the park. After Disneyland closes for the evening, cast members spread throughout the park, conducting point-by-point inspections of motors, electrical connections, relays, fuses, sound systems,

Divers inspect underwater mechanical effects and tracking rails just after sunrise in the waterways of the Jungle Cruise where charging hippos usually lurk during the day (opposite page).

Disneyland is an exercise in perpetual renewal: an Astro Orbiter ride vehicle receives an after-hours touch-up (above), while the marble floors of the Plaza Inn restaurant are buffed to a bright shine (left).

In the still of the night a Facilities and Maintenance crew replaces the rim lights along Main Street (opposite page).

The backstage artisans of Disneyland possess many unique skills, including aging and graining facades (below top) and restoring the antique horses of King Arthur Carrousel (below bottom).

and lighting. This preventive maintenance is essential to ensure the reliable and safe operations of the park's attractions during the day.

Also at night, electricians from Facilities and Maintenance inspect some of the more than 100,000 lightbulbs used in Disneyland® Park, including the 11,000 rim lights used to outline the buildings on Main Street, U.S.A. All the twinkling lights on Main Street are replaced when the bulbs reach 80 percent of their expected life.

The Facilities and Maintenance teams have some of the more unique jobs in the park. Occasionally, the maintenance team gives the Matterhorn a new coat of "snow" and also a wash down with soap and water to keep it gleaming white. The team has also developed an uncommon knowledge of 19th-century machinery with the complete overhaul of the authentic Mark Twain Riverboat and the genuine steam trains of the Disneyland Railroad.

Over time members of the Facilities and Maintenance teams have become masters of paint and gilding as well. More than 20,000 gallons of paint are used each year to give the park a better-than-new look, keeping landmarks such as the brightly colored skyline of Mickey's Toontown in vibrant shape. And the Facilities and Maintenance teams also keep the 14-karat-gold gilding that adorns the turrets of Sleeping Beauty Castle, the mechanisms of Dumbo the Flying Elephant, and the spires of "it's a small world" gleaming year round.

The versatility of the Facilities and Maintenance teams extends to maintaining the functionality of the park's various Audio-Animatronics® cast members, including the rambunctious cast of Pirates of the Caribbean and the 16th president of the United States, Mr. Lincoln. This involves frequent checks for wear and tear and accuracy in the animation. Occasionally, Disneyland make-up artists, costumers, and hairdressers give these special cast members complete makeovers.

At Disneyland old-time craftsmanship and work integrity are still fashionable assets. Virtually every craft imaginable is practiced at Disneyland, including woodcarving, glass blowing, sign making, sculpting, mural painting, weaving, model-making, ship rigging, and saddle making.

In the backstage workshops, artisans apply their skills and talents to create authentic items such as bridles, horseshoes, fused-glass windows, miniatures, and etched signage. They also decorate the park's fanciful shop windows, and provide the impressive interior décor seen throughout Disneyland. Although not readily noticeable, the behind-the-scenes magic of Disneyland is subliminally appreciated by the countless guests who visit the park year after year.

MEMORIES OF A LIFETIME

As guests walk into Disneyland® Park they pass under the entrance archways of the Main Street Station. Over each archway is a brass plaque that reads "Here You Leave Today and Enter the World of Yesterday, Tomorrow and

HERE YOU LEAVE TODAY AND ENTER THE WORLD OF YESTERDAY, TOMORROW AND FANTASY

Fantasy." However, it could be added that guests also enter a world of wonderful memories—for Disneyland is indeed a place where memories of a life-time are made every day. At the end of a visit, a little Disney magic leaves with each guest.

The Mulan Parade delights guests along Main Street with its impressive floats, colorful costumes, and authentic Chinese performers (above).

The Party Gras Parade, staged in celebration of the park's 35th anniversary, featured lively calypso music and six 37-foot-tall Disney character inflatable balloon floats (opposite page).

The beloved Main Street Electrical Parade (following pages) premiered at Disneyland in 1972 and quickly became the most popular parade ever staged at a Disney theme park. The parade was officially retired in 1996 after more than 3,500 performances over a 24-year run.

Let Us Entertain You

Since Disneyland® Park opened in 1955, live entertainment has been as much a part of the landscape of the park as Sleeping Beauty Castle or the Matterhorn. Disneyland has a rich history of presenting state-of-the-art parades and spectaculars, colorful fireworks presentations, first-rate musical performances, rollicking stage shows, and, of course, appearances by the beloved Disney characters.

The Disneyland entertainment legacy literally began on opening day with what would become an entertainment tradition at Disneyland—parades. On that hot July day many years ago, Disneyland presented its very first parade down Main Street, U.S.A. Led by Walt Disney and some of the opening day dignitaries, the parade was high in energy and charming in its simplicity.

Disneyland has since led the way in creating some of the most impressive parade pageants presented anywhere in the world. Whether celebrating special occasions, holidays, or one of the beloved Disney animated films, Disneyland parades have delighted millions of park guests from virtually every corner of the globe.

Utilizing state-of-the-art sound systems, music integration, lighting, float construction, and motion picture projection effects, Disneyland® Park parades have made Main Street, U.S.A. one of the largest outdoor entertainment venues, and certainly one of the most traversed parade routes, in the country. Through the years these parades have featured performers from all over the world and have become an integral part of the Disneyland experience.

In addition to the daily parades, another Disneyland tradition is providing guests with a wide variety of live musical performances throughout the park. This tradition can also be traced back to opening day when the Disneyland Band first marched down Main Street.

Originally hired for a two-week engagement, the Disneyland Band has logged over 3,500 marching miles and nearly 75,000 performances over the past 45 years. With a repertoire of over 400 numbers, the Disneyland Band continues to provide the main musical soundtrack for "The Happiest Place on Earth."

The Dapper Dans are another regular feature of the Disneyland musical landscape, an ever-harmonious quartet that greets guests to Main Street, U.S.A. Whether harmonizing on "My Coney Island Baby" or spreading holiday cheer with a chorus of hand-held chiming bells, the Dapper Dans generate delight up and down Main Street with their musical escapades.

Further up Main Street, guests frequently gather around the shimmering white upright piano at Coke Corner to hear the ragtime sounds of the Coke Corner Pianist. With lightning speed he tickles the ivories to produce toe-tapping renditions of

The joyous Lion King Celebration captivates guests along Main Street, U.S.A. with its inspiring music and high-energy performers (opposite page).

Disneyland is renowned for its live music, such as the popular Disneyland Band (left) and the jazz bands of New Orleans Square (below top).

The Genie towers over guests during a performance of Aladdin's Royal Caravan (below bottom).

classic Disney tunes and turn-of-the-century favorites to the delight of guests of all ages.

At Disneyland® Park, it's just a short walk from the marching bands, parades, and ragtime sounds of Main Street, U.S.A. to the jungle rhythms of Adventureland. Would-be adventure-seekers in this tropical outpost are easily distracted from their travels by a captivating steel-drum calypso beat or the musical sounds of South America as performed on authentic native instruments of the region.

In New Orleans Square, Dixieland music reigns supreme. From the sublime and smooth jazz tunes of the Royal Street Bachelors to the energetic Side Street Strutters, New Orleans

is the place for true jazz aficionados. On the narrow pathways and in the ornate courtyards of New Orleans Square guests can also discover a variety of entertaining mimes, tap dancers, and street-corner musicians.

As guests venture into the backwoods wilderness of Critter Country and the bustling western riverfront of Frontierland, the sounds of bluegrass and country-western music permeate the air.

Inside the swinging doors of the Golden Horseshoe saloon, guests can witness the uproarious antics of Benny Hill and the Hillbillies or experience the acts of an Old West variety show. Outside in front of the Southwest landscape of Big Thunder Mountain, guests may also thrill to authentic Mexican mariachi music from south of the border.

Just a short walk over the drawbridge of Sleeping Beauty Castle is Tinker Bell Toy Shoppe, where guests can relax while one of the Disney princesses reads aloud an entertaining and familiar fairy tale. Outside in the courtyard, would-be kings can try their hand at removing the sword Excalibur from its resting place with the help of Merlin the Wizard in The Sword in the Stone Ceremony.

At the Fantasyland Theater guests will find elaborate musical stage shows, presented throughout the year, featuring singers, dancers, and the lovable Disney characters. During the holiday season, the Fantasyland Theater hosts the inspiring Disneyland® Christmas Candlelight Ceremony and Processional. Accompanied by a live orchestra and massed chorus of over 800 voices, the ceremony features a celebrity guest narrator in a moving presentation of the traditional Christmas story.

In Tomorrowland, the unique Tomorrowland Terrace Stage literally rises out of the ground to present contemporary sounds in rock and roll. Guests may also encounter the irreverent and energetic Trash Can Trio, who find musical percussion inspiration in their bright and shining trash bins.

During the day at the Plaza Gardens Stage in the Plaza Hub, guests can enjoy performances by the many guest groups that visit the park. From college and high school bands and choruses to community groups from across the country, the Plaza Gardens has played host to countless visiting entertainers, including such big band legends as Count Basie, Harry James, Woody Herman, Les Brown, and Lionel Hampton.

The summer nighttime tradition of "Fantasy in the Sky" fireworks over Disneyland® Park began in 1956. Since then nearly 4,000 performances of this show have been presented. Utilizing over 200 shells carrying 400 pounds of explosives, each show features the finest fireworks available, many of them imported from China, Japan, France, Germany, and Australia.

In 1992 a new tradition in Disneyland®
Park nighttime entertainment made its
debut—Fantasmic! Easily one of the
most complex and technically advanced
shows ever presented at a Disney
theme park, this hugely popular evening
extravaganza features a battle of good
and evil inside Mickey Mouse's fanciful
imagination.

Statistics:

•12,000 guests can view the show along
the shores of the Rivers of America in
Frontierland.

•More than 100 cast and crew members
are needed to stage one presentation of
the show.

•341 costumes are necessary in order to
present the show seven nights a week.

•Three 30-foot-tall by 50-foot-wide mist
screens are used in the show; 70 mm
film images are projected onto the
screens via projectors stationed on Tom
Sawyer's Island.

•The 45-foot-tall Sleeping Beauty Dragon
breathes fire, setting the river aflame.

During the year Disneyland plays host to numerous visiting high school, college, and community marching bands and choirs from throughout the United States and from around the world. Their enthusiastic performances provide festive entertainment for guests of all ages (above).

Disneyland Around the Seasons

In the temperate Mediterranean climate of Southern California the change of seasons is seldom obvious. With an average year-round temperature of 72 degrees and no extreme changes in climate, the turning of the year seems less pronounced in the warm California sunshine.

However, in the magical oasis of Disneyland® Park, where virtually anything is possible, the changing seasons and their associated holidays are welcomed and celebrated with enthusiasm. Although every day at Disneyland is carefree, the seasons and holidays bring special nuances and festivities that add an extra layer of enchantment to the Magic Kingdom.

Springtime comes quickly to Disneyland, usually arriving in early March. The park seems to explode with color as the flower beds herald the arrival of spring with an ever-blooming array of colorful flowers. During this time of year you may be able to spot the Easter Bunny at the Disneyland Resort hotels and in the park, and even an April shower can make a rare appearance. There is no place quite like Disneyland in the springtime, when bright sunny skies are dotted with puffy white clouds and the aroma of flowers fills the air.

From Memorial Day through Labor Day, when the days turn hot and the nights are warm, Disneyland® Park takes on a patriotic spirit. Red, white, and blue ribbons and bunting decorate Main Street and the Plaza Hub. Every day visiting marching bands from around the world perform on Main Street, U.S.A., and the Disneyland Collegiate All-Star Band provides energetic entertainment before the nightly parade. In the evening the traditional Fantasy in the Sky fireworks spectacular sets the summer skies ablaze over Sleeping Beauty Castle.

Autumn weaves its own spell over the Magic Kingdom. Suddenly, jack-o'-lanterns, scarecrows, and swirling leaves seem to pop up overnight in Town Square and the Plaza Hub. The evenings turn cool and the orange twilight skies over the Disneyland skyline announce that Halloween and Thanksgiving are on their way. Feasts for Thanksgiving are prepared to perfection at special dinners throughout the Disneyland Resort Hotels, while restaurants inside the park provide traditional favorites as well.

Winter immediately follows Thanksgiving at Disneyland. Suddenly, "The Happiest Place on Earth" is transformed into "The Merriest Place on Earth," as the park greets the holidays

Main Street, U.S.A. is the perfect backdrop for numerous patriotic festivities, such as a celebration of the Bill of Rights (below left).

Mr. and Mrs. Easter Bunny don their finest Sunday apparel to make springtime appearances at the Disneyland Resort hotels, much to the delight of eager young guests (below right).

with a stunning array of decorations, seasonal foods, shows, parades, and festivities. From Main Street, U.S.A. to Mickey's Toontown, Disneyland® Park is aglow with holiday cheer.

Guests on Main Street, U.S.A. are greeted by the pine aroma and impressive sight of a 60-foot-tall Christmas tree in Town Square. Every year the Disneyland Landscaping team handpicks the tree fresh from the pine forests of Mt. Shasta in Northern California. It takes two weeks for a team of cast members to decorate the tree, to cover it with more than 8,000 colorful lights and traditional Victorian ornaments.

Up and down Main Street, guests are enticed by the smell of brewing Christmas cider, freshly made popcorn balls, and gingerbread cookies. Sharp-eyed guests will notice that each store on Main Street is decorated with its own distinctive wreaths and ornaments. As a personal touch, a little Christmas tree is showcased and illuminated throughout the holidays in the window of Walt Disney's apartment above the Main Street Fire Station.

Main Street townsfolk stroll the lanes and charm Disneyland guests with traditional Christmas carols and tales of holidays past. In the afternoon the spectacular sights and sounds of the Christmas Fantasy Parade, which features over 120 performers, thrills young and old alike. This Disneyland holiday tradition incorporates live music, beautiful costumes, prancing reindeer, many of the lovable Disney characters, and an appearance by Santa Claus himself.

At the end of Main Street lies Sleeping Beauty Castle, whose splendid regal holiday décor includes elegant medieval ornamentation and soft flickering lanterns. The spires are

Mickey Mouse wreaths decorate Main Street, U.S.A. (above), marching Toy Soldiers lead off the annual Christmas parade (below right), and Mickey's Toontown greets the season with a touch of cartoon whimsy (below left).

New Orleans Square gets jazzed up for the holidays (opposite page).

153

festooned with garlands reminiscent of the briar rose featured so prominently in the timeless fairy tale.

Guests who prefer their holidays with a jazz beat need wander no further than New Orleans Square. Here the Crescent City has been energized for the holidays with the sights, sounds, and tastes of a French-Quarter Christmas. Winter masquerade and southern holiday delicacies create an atmosphere of fun and merriment, all accompanied by holiday tunes served up "N'awlins" style and performed in flavors of Cajun, Zydeco, and Jazz. On the balconies and in the alleyways and winding streets of New Orleans Square, holiday wreaths reflect Mardi Gras motifs, while the holiday garlands and decorations feature beautiful angels, comical alligators, and smiling crescent moons.

In the backwoods of Critter Country, the wily and exuberant bruins of the Country Bear Christmas Special perform a toe-tapping musical holiday hoedown. And over in Adventureland and Frontierland the holiday decorations display the far-off wilderness and tropical motifs of each land, incorporating tropical fruits, colorful flowers, corn husk garlands, luminaries, natural wood wreaths, berries, nuts, and pine cones.

The local residents of Mickey's Toontown decorate their homes for the holidays with a colorful, animated flair, providing a whimsical cartoon approach to the holidays at every turn. A 16-foot-tall Christmas tree in front of Toon Hall is draped with oversized "Toony" ornaments and a top-heavy topper that gives the tree a comical sway. Lamppost wreaths in Town Square feature Mickey's signature ears. Wacky, short-circuiting lights flash from the Electric Company garland, while firecrackers and fireworks explode from the Fireworks Factory garland.

Finally, in Fantasyland, the annual "it's a small world" Holiday spectacular transforms the beloved attraction into a breathtaking wintertime celebration. Intertwining such popular holiday tunes as "Jingle Bells" and "Deck the Halls" with the familiar strains of "it's a small world," the attraction whimsically showcases the holiday traditions of many lands.

Nearly a half million sparkling lights illuminate the entrance mall and international skyline of "it's a small world" Holiday. In addition, the famous clock tower and topiaries are decorated with Santa hats and red bows. As guests approach the attraction, they are welcomed by 13 international holiday wreaths—each one displaying a traditional holiday greeting in a different language.

Every season in Disneyland® Park has a distinct and special appeal. Through the years the various holidays celebrated at the park have become highly anticipated events for many of the millions of guests who annually visit the Magic Kingdom. Over the past four and a half decades holiday time at Disneyland has become as much a cherished family tradition as pumpkin pie, fireworks, and mistletoe.

Holiday fireworks light up the nighttime sky over Sleeping Beauty Castle (opposite page).

Santa Claus greets guests during the Christmas Fantasy Parade (below top).

A brilliant fusion of light and color transforms the entrance to "it's a small world" Holiday (below bottom).

Main Street glows with holiday spirit (following pages).

Orville Redenbacher's® Popcorn can be found throughout the park and is one of the most popular snacks in the Magic Kingdom (above). Families who visit the park will find a variety of treats and menus to delight every tastebud (below). Mickey Mouse, ever the gracious host, displays some mouthwatering desserts straight from the kitchens of New Orleans Square (right). As guests wander down Main Street they are likely to be enticed by the tantalizing aroma of freshly baked goods. One of the most popular confections is to be found at the Blue Ribbon® Bakery—enormous really sticky sticky buns (opposite page). These gooey delights are best accompanied by one of the gourmet coffees also available at the bakery.

Something's Always Cooking in the Park

Disneyland® Park is known around the world as "The Happiest Place on Earth." However, it could also be called "The Magic Kingdom of Culinary Delights." A vast array of culinary pleasures sure to satisfy every appetite are to be found throughout the eight themed lands of Disneyland.

Long-time guests to Disneyland are bound to have a favorite treat, meal, or snack they associate with the park. For some it might be the distinct air-popped taste of Orville Redenbacher's popcorn (found throughout the park), the sugary sweetness of a warm churro (found in the Plaza Hub), or the creamy decadence of "Fantasia" ice cream (a concoction of burgundy cherries, pistachios, and banana ice cream found only at the

Gibson Girl Ice Cream Parlor). Still others might crave a freshly baked really sticky sticky bun (Blue Ribbon Bakery on Main Street), a tangy pineapple whip (The Tiki Juice Bar in Adventureland), or a cool green mint julep (The Mint Julep Bar in New Orleans Square).

Not only is your imagination allowed to run wild at Disneyland® Park but so are your tastebuds. Inside the park there are over 30 unique eateries that can satisfy even the most discerning tastes. On Main Street guests can watch the world go by from their sidewalk table at the Carnation Café or they can dine in Victorian elegance at the Plaza Inn. For those who need to satisfy a sweet tooth, the famous Blue Ribbon® Bakery can come to the rescue with its assortment of delicious, freshly baked muffins, scones, and gourmet coffees.

Beyond Main Street guests can sample delicacies from many far-off lands. In Adventureland, explorers of all ages can savor the mouthwatering delights of the Bengal Barbecue or enjoy fresh tropical fruit at the Indy Fruit Cart. While in Frontierland western thrill-seekers can chow down on fresh barbecued ribs and chicken at Big Thunder Barbecue.

In New Orleans Square, guests dine under an umbrella of constant midnight sky in the Blue Bayou Restaurant, where hearty appetites can enjoy the restaurant's famous Monte Cristo sandwiches or the creamy clam chowder. Guests to the Blue

Bayou experience romantic moonlit dining all day long, and the intriguing atmosphere is enlivened by the sight of dancing fireflies and the occasional shooting star.

The Mint Julep Bar is the place for pastry delights like authentic warm and sugary southern-style fritters. And for those who prefer their meals with a backwoods flavor, the Hungry Bear Restaurant in Critter Country provides a tranquil setting along the Rivers of America.

Guests at Mickey's Toontown will find that the food fare is presented with a little more character—such as Clarabelle's Frozen Yogurt, Daisy's Diner, and Pluto's Dog House (serving hot dogs of course). For a touch of whimsy guests need look no further than the Bavarian-themed Village Haus in Fantasyland, where the adventures of Pinocchio are depicted in delightful carvings and detailed murals.

There's no better stop than Redd Rockett's Pizza Port in Tomorrowland for meals with an out-of-this-world flair. Space travelers with a galaxy-size hunger will easily find the solid and liquid fuel at Redd Rockett's appealing. Menu choices include Mars-inara Pasta, Terra Nova Tomato Basil Pasta, Planetary Pizza Salad, and Starfield of Greens Salad.

Disneyland® Park guests are offered a wide array of dining choices. At the Blue Bayou Restaurant in New Orleans Square, guests dine under a perpetual canopy of nighttime sky (above), while modern-day space rangers can grab a quick bite at Redd Rockett's Pizza Port in Tomorrowland (below). Guests who like to eat in the great outdoors can enjoy authentic western chuckwagon fare at Big Thunder Barbecue (right).

Shopping with a "Disney" Touch

One of the many aspects of Disneyland® Park that helps make it such a rich experience time and again is the diversity of choices guests have when they enter the Magic Kingdom. Some guests choose to immediately seek out the many adventures and attractions, while others want to quickly satisfy a hearty appetite with a Magic Kingdom food specialty. However, there are also those who enter Disneyland with one thing on their mind—shopping.

Disneyland is a shopper's paradise, with treasures of all kinds for young and old alike. It is at Disneyland where the famed Mickey Mouse ears really became a standard accessory, beginning in the mid 1950s. More than half a million Mickey Mouse ears are sold annually at the park. Additionally, Disneyland is the birthplace of the Mickey Mouse balloon—a popular and unique novelty created in various pastel shades and easily identified by the three round inflatable sections that form the famous three circles of Mickey's silhouette.

Frequent guests to Disneyland will notice that the merchandise offered throughout the park changes seasonally, reflecting new styles, holiday themes, and special events. Most of the

Mickey Mouse is well represented in the many shops of Disneyland (above). Throughout the park guests can find a variety of merchandise and souvenirs featuring Mickey Mouse and other popular Disney characters.

park's shopping activity occurs on Main Street, U.S.A. Here guests can find a variety of merchandise easily accessible within the interconnecting shops up and down the fanciful lane. As a matter of fact, many noted city planners, architects, and authors have argued that Main Street, U.S.A. at Disneyland® Park is the original forerunner of today's modern shopping mall.

Over the past 45 years, Disneyland has become a shopping destination for many of the park's frequent guests. Whether shopping for souvenirs or hunting for the perfect gift, Disneyland guests can find an impressive array of merchandise throughout the eight themed lands.

The itinerary of any serious shopper at Disneyland should include a trip to the Emporium on Main Street. Famous for its detailed animated window displays highlighting scenes from

The Silhouette Studio on Main Street provides Disneyland guests with unique turn-of-the-century souvenirs (above).

Watches with a little character (literally) can be found at New Century Timepieces on Main Street (below).

Beautiful pieces of crystal illuminate the interior of the Cristal d'Orleans shop in New Orleans Square (right).

The Mickey Mouse balloon has become a symbol synonymous with Disneyland. Created in a broad assortment of colors, the Mickey Mouse balloon is a popular end-of-day souvenir for young Mouseketeers (left).

At the Candy Kitchen on Main Street guests can purchase candy confections that are made from scratch daily (below).

classic Disney animated films, the Emporium features a wide array of items, including clothing and souvenirs, many of which are available only at Disneyland® Park.

Other Main Street stores and shops feature such eclectic items as hand-blown glass creations (Crystal Arts), hand-cut silhouettes (Silhouette Studio), candy confections made daily by master candy-makers (Candy Palace and Candy Kitchen), and one-of-a-kind watches featuring hand-drawn images of Disney characters and Disneyland icons (New Century Timepieces).

Main Street is very much rooted in nostalgia for the past and so it is appropriate that it is home to two unique shops that celebrate the desire for all things Disney. At the Disneyana Shop, avid Disney collectors of all ages can browse among the displays of popular Disney collectibles such as images of Walt Disney Animation Art, the award-winning Walt Disney Classics Collection, and exclusive-to-Disneyland posters, books, sculptures, and watches.

At the 20th Century Music Company, guests can relive their visits to Disneyland by creating their very own compact disc compilations of popular sounds and music from the Magic Kingdom. Featuring tracks from the Disneyland of yesteryear to current popular shows and attractions, the Disneyland Forever kiosks provide guests with an unforgettable audio trip down a memory lane of their own making.

New Orleans Square is another popular locale for shopping within the Magic Kingdom. As guests enter the square, they encounter Port de Orleans, a lively mart that features items imported directly from Louisiana, such as a variety of spicy Cajun sauces, beignet mixes, and coffees with chicory. The shop also offers items derived

from two of the signature attractions of New Orleans Square—Pirates of the Caribbean and the Haunted Mansion.

The ornate courtyards and winding streets of New Orleans Square boast some of the park's most distinctive shops. Guests can discover one-of-a-kind pieces of estate jewelry at Jewel of Orleans, have customized parasols decorated at the Parasol Cart, or have their portrait rendered in pastels by the Portrait Artists. In La Boutique de Noel, guests can find a wide array of Disney holiday decorative items, while La Mascarade d'Orleans features high-end antiques and collectibles.

Perhaps the most distinctive shop in all of Disneyland® Park is The Disney Gallery. Located above the Pirates of the Caribbean adventure in New Orleans Square, the gallery location was originally designed as a large, private apartment for Walt Disney and his family, serving as a larger complement to Walt's original Disneyland studio apartment located above the Fire Station on Main Street.

Furnished in 19th-century style, and equipped with a climate-controlled patio and an electronic intercom entry, the New Orleans Square apartment was intended to be used by Walt and his family as a place where they could stay the night at the park and entertain visiting dignitaries and business associates. When Walt passed away in 1966 the apartment was just nearing completion and he never saw it finished.

Today, however, The Disney Gallery serves as a showcase for the artwork of Walt Disney Imagineering. Here guests can buy original or limited-edition images of Disneyland® Park attraction designs, posters, and concept art. Throughout the year the gallery hosts a series of events and art signings, many of the them featuring some of the original Disney Imagineers who helped to create the park.

All through Disneyland guests will find an abundance of merchandise sure to appeal to every interest—from the jungle-themed exports of Adventureland, to the western apparel of Frontierland, to the gadgets and gizmos of Tomorrowland, to the storybooks and dolls of Fantasyland. During the year numerous special events are held at various stores and shops in the park, featuring personal appearances by noted authors, sculptors, doll-makers, artists, and celebrities.

Bonanza Outfitters in Frontierland offers western wear for all pioneering excursions (above).

Some of the most popular Disneyland souvenirs are the cuddly Disney character plush toys, such as the always charming Minnie Mouse (left).

Port d'Orleans in New Orleans Square provides shoppers with authentic treasures from down south "N'awlins" way (opposite page).

Everybody Comes to Disneyland

The official hotels of the Disneyland Resort—the original award-winning Disneyland Hotel and the contemporary Disneyland Pacific Hotel—are situated on 65 acres adjacent to Disneyland® Park. Since the late 1950s, the Disneyland Resort hotels have literally grown up in the shadow of the Magic Kingdom.

The Disneyland Hotel first welcomed guests in 1955 and eventually blossomed into a world-renowned 1,100-room resort destination. The 502-room Disneyland Pacific Hotel joined the Disneyland Resort in 1995. Today the hotels provide families with deluxe accommodations, a wide range of restaurants and shops, and recreational opportunities.

By purchasing a Disneyland Passport, Disneyland Resort guests can enjoy early admission into Disneyland up to an hour and a half before the general public for each day of their stay. They also have quick access to Disneyland via the Disneyland Monorail, which has an exclusive station stop right at the doorstep of the resort's shopping and dining area, providing round-trip service directly into the heart of Tomorrowland.

The Disneyland® Resort hotels offer numerous restaurants and lounges, ranging from great family-style dining with a Disney flair at Goofy's Kitchen, to the award-winning Granville's Steak House, to the new Hook's Pointe & Wine Cellar. Delicious teriyaki and tempura dishes are served at Yamabuki, the resort's authentic Japanese restaurant, while fresh California cuisine can be found at Disney's PCH Grill. There's even a Coffee House at both hotels, featuring specialty coffees and fresh-baked pastries.

One of the centerpieces of the Disneyland Resort is the 40,000-square-foot Never Land aquatic area, inspired by Walt Disney's animated classic *Peter Pan*. The 5,000-square-foot swimming pool, with its winding shoreline, depicts the lagoon from the film, accented by the distinctive Skull Rock, Hangman's Tree, and a backdrop of the Misty Mountains.

Near the pool is Captain Hook's galleon and a comical sculpture, the hungry crocodile always on the lookout for Captain Hook. A spacious bubbling spa is themed after the Mermaid Lagoon, complete with the figure of a mermaid sitting at water's edge.

Guests of any age who want to make a splashy entrance can follow a trail that winds its way up the slopes of the Misty Mountains, continues across a wood-and-rope suspension

The impressive Disneyland Hotel has been one of Southern California's top resort hotel destinations for over four decades. Amid blooming flowers, the Bonita Tower of the Disneyland Hotel stands against the bright California sunshine (opposite page).

The elegant Granville's Steak House is one of the many award-winning restaurants featured at the Disneyland Resort hotels (above).

Exquisite banquet and ballroom facilities are available at the Disneyland® Resort hotels (above and below).

Disneyland Pacific Hotel guests enjoy tea with Mary Poppins (above right).

Watery adventure awaits in the Never Land Pool at the Disneyland Hotel (right).

bridge, and leads to the 14-foot-high headwaters of the pool. Here, guests embark on a thrilling, 100-foot-long water slide that rushes through Skull Rock and culminates in an exciting plunge into the lagoon.

The palm-tree-dotted shores surrounding the pool offer ample space for guests to sunbathe and relax on chaise lounges, and the nearby Captain's Galley offers salads, sandwiches, and beverages. Complementing the fantasy atmosphere of the Never Land area is the always-popular nighttime aquatic ballets of the Fantasy Waters show.

The Disneyland Hotel and the Disneyland Pacific Hotel are connected by a landscaped walkway, providing easy access for guests of either property so they may enjoy the benefits of both hotels. Recreational opportunities available throughout the beautifully landscaped resort include a choice of three swimming pools, a tropical sandy beach, and waterfalls and koi ponds perfect for leisurely strolls.

Of course, one of the most important benefits of staying at the Disneyland® Resort hotels is the chance to meet the Disney characters at meals served daily in both hotels. Families enjoy tableside visits, photo opportunities, or old-fashioned hugs with one of the Disney characters.

Roaming around the resort are the Bell Hops, a zany musical crew who set up stage pretty much any place they like, to the immense delight of resort guests who can join in the fun. Shopping at the resort's impressive variety of shops is another magical experience, with everything from resort fashions to Disney souvenirs.

Families looking for a special level of service can elect to stay in one of the resort's concierge-level rooms, with upgraded amenities and complimentary access to the exclusive concierge lounges, featuring continental breakfast and evening wine and cheese. In addition to deluxe guestrooms, the resort offers suites ranging from 740 to 3,400 square feet. Meetings and conventions are also easily accommodated within the resort's 180,00 square feet of meeting and banquet space.

Thundering waterfalls cascade into serene koi ponds beneath the Marina Tower at the Disneyland Hotel (above).

Hook's Pointe (below left) and the PCH Grill (below right), two of the flagship restaurants of the Disneyland Resort hotels, offer guests an array of fine seafood specialities and innovative California cuisine.

The Heartbeat of the Magic Kingdom

The heartbeat of Disneyland® Park is to be found in the more than six generations of guests and cast members from all points of the globe who have grown up with Disneyland, making it a part of the world's collective consciousness. It is a place built upon emotions and memories. Virtually everyone has a Disneyland story to tell—everyone from commoners to kings.

A favorite Disneyland memory can be as simple as recalling your very first trip to the park. For others their memories might include a special encounter with one of the lovable Disney characters or being awestruck by a particular parade or show. For some the most memorable experience may have been when they went to Disneyland and were finally tall enough to drive their own Autopia car.

A happy couple celebrates their marriage in the elegant and romantic shadow of Sleeping Beauty Castle (above top). Minnie Mouse makes a new friend in the Magic Kingdom (above bottom), a toddler shows off his enthusiasm for the park in a most unique fashion (left), and another Disney memory to last a lifetime is created (opposite page).

The memories are many and varied. Over the years more than 3.2 million students from more than 16,000 senior classes have celebrated their high school graduation at Disneyland® Park. For some the park was the chosen backdrop for their first date or the landmark where they stole their first kiss. Disneyland holds special significance for the countless couples who have proposed marriage or exchanged wedding vows in the romantic shadow of Sleeping Beauty Castle.

Through the decades, generations of families and friends have shared special times together at Disneyland. It has become one of life's benchmarks, captured forever, most likely, in treasured photographs that instantly rekindle happy times in the company of beloved friends, moms and dads, brothers, sisters, grandparents, cousins, uncles, and aunts.

Disneyland is also where major sports figures go to celebrate, as showcased in a number of memorable TV commercials (" . . . you've just won the Super Bowl. What are you going to do now?" asks the announcer. "I'm going to Disneyland!" exclaims the victor). The park is where grown-ups shed the pretense of adulthood and indulge themselves in childhood pleasures (at Disneyland adults in silly hats are always in fashion). In turn, when children visit Disneyland they savor the opportunity of being in a realm free of the rules and regulations found in the everyday world of grown-ups.

In 1993 the Plaza Hub of Disneyland saw the dedication of a bronze statue of Walt Disney and Mickey Mouse entitled "Partners" (the first of its kind placed in any of the Disney theme parks). Inscribed on a plaque at the base of the statue is a quote from Walt Disney that succinctly sums up the possible secret to the success of Disneyland: "Most of all what I want Disneyland to be is a happy place—where parents and children can have fun together."

Mickey and Minnie Mouse are the official hosts of Disneyland, greeting countless guests yearly throughout the park as well as starring in numerous parades and shows (above top).

Captain Hook's first mate, Mr. Smee, finds a new pirate recruit in Fantasyland (above bottom).

Mickey's faithful pal Pluto puts a smile on the face of a young admirer (right).

Walt Disney delights some young admirers with a visit in front of Sleeping Beauty Castle (opposite page).

"There will never be another Disneyland"

In the mid-1960s, as Walt Disney entered the twilight of his life and embarked on the planning and creation of the Walt Disney World® Resort in Florida, he commented that "There will never be another Disneyland."

This simple fact has remained true over the past 45 years. For all the expansion and change that has come to pass at Disneyland® Park, along with the creation of other Disney theme parks around the globe, Disneyland has retained an extremely special and unique place within The Walt Disney Company and the world at large.

The initial impact that Disneyland made on American culture, and its continued influence on popular culture at large, cannot be underestimated. The legend and lore of Disneyland has been celebrated in numerous books, documentaries, and magazine articles. The park has been invoked in numerous popular songs and has been the location for the filming of two major motion pictures.

In its early formative years, respected urban planners, noted architects, and futurists hailed Disneyland for its groundbreaking design and use of detail to convey themes. "In Disneyland, he [Disney] has proven again that the first function of architecture is to make men over, make them wish to go on living, feed fresh oxygen, grow them tall, delight their eyes, make them kind," declared Ray Bradbury, famed science fiction writer and futurist, in the early 1960s. "Disneyland liberates men to their better selves."

Further evidence of its ongoing importance as a cultural icon was a recent critically acclaimed touring exhibition entitled "The Architecture of Reassurance" (1997–99), which displayed many of the original designs and concept sketches utilized to create Disneyland. According to cultural historian Karal Ann Marling, Disneyland is the "most complex, baffling, and beloved work of art produced in postwar America."

Senator John F. Kennedy visits Disneyland in the early 1960s (above top).

Mamie and President Eisenhower take a spin on the Main Street Fire Engine (above middle).

Vice President Richard M. Nixon and family help Walt Disney officially open the Disneyland Monorail (above bottom).

President Truman and his wife Bess enjoy a leisurely ride aboard a Main Street Horse-drawn Streetcar (above right).

By welcoming over 400 million guests during the past four decades, Disneyland® Park has solidified its status as an international destination and world institution. Since 1955 Disneyland has hosted some of the 20th century's most prominent dignitaries, including heads of state (counting seven U.S. presidents), sports figures, and entertainment celebrities. But more importantly, guests from virtually every country and every walk of life have embraced Disneyland as their own. There are currently over 51,000 pages on the World Wide Web, along with over 120 Web sites, that either mention Disneyland or are dedicated to the original Magic Kingdom.

The name Disneyland has become so universally recognized that it has been used to introduce new audiences in Japan (Tokyo Disneyland) and France (Disneyland Paris) to the Disney theme park experience. But even with the new Disney theme parks guests still flock to the park that started it all.

"Like most youngsters in the post-World War II years, I grew up watching Mickey and Donald and Goofy and 'The Wonderful World of Disney,'" recalls Michael Eisner, chairman and chief executive officer of The Walt Disney Company. "But Disneyland was an impossible dream. In those days, thirteen-year-old New York kids didn't travel cross-country to live out their fantasies, not even in the world's greatest theme park."

"Years later, as tourists, my wife Jane and I finally entered the gates of the Magic Kingdom," Eisner says. "Whatever youthful images I'd once conjured up were dwarfed by the beauty and spectacle of the place. The reality was better than the illusion."

"That was well over twenty years ago," Eisner adds. "Sad to say, I'm no longer able to look at Disneyland through the eyes of a visitor. The park that once was solely my pleasure is now part of my job. Today there are other, newer Disney theme parks—in Florida, in Japan, in France—but Disneyland remains our flagship. Everything we've built since 1955 is a reflection of its creative spirit. Most of our best new ideas still get their start in the original Magic Kingdom."

Disneyland® Park helped to introduce to the world a whole new concept in outdoor entertainment—the Disney theme park. As the first Disney theme park, Disneyland has produced numerous technological breakthroughs in entertainment, design, and transportation that have been emulated throughout the entertainment industry and in urban planning.

Innovations pioneered at Disneyland include the first daily operating monorail system in the Western Hemisphere; Matterhorn Bobsleds, the first themed roller-coaster in the world, and the first attraction of its kind to use cylindrical rails and urethane wheels, which are now standard on attractions of this type; Walt Disney's Enchanted Tiki Room, which introduced the world to the wonders of Audio-Animatronics® technology, an electro-mechanical system that combines synchronized sound and movement to create three-dimensional animation; and the first daily operating PeopleMover system in the United States.

As guests to Disneyland enter the park under the trestles of the Main Street Station, they pass under two little-noticed brass plaques that read: "Here You Leave Today and Enter the World of Yesterday, Tomorrow and Fantasy." However, one little bit of information is missing on those plaques. Guests to Disneyland also enter into a unique realm of magic that has yet to be exactly replicated anywhere else. There is indeed a special magic at Disneyland that transcends the encroachment of contemporary styles, fads, and trends.

Although the park continues to expand and change, it also continues to success-fully retain its own special character. As the only Disney theme park created under the direct supervision of Walt Disney himself, the park still possesses many nuances that can be directly attributed to him. Perhaps that's one of the many reasons why "there will never be another Disneyland."